Altered States

Altered States

Changing Populations, Changing Parties, and the Transformation of the American Political Landscape

THOMAS M. HOLBROOK

OXFORD
UNIVERSITY PRESS

Oxford University Press is a department of the University of Oxford. It furthers
the University's objective of excellence in research, scholarship, and education
by publishing worldwide. Oxford is a registered trade mark of Oxford University
Press in the UK and certain other countries.

Published in the United States of America by Oxford University Press
198 Madison Avenue, New York, NY 10016, United States of America.

Library of Congress Cataloging-in-Publication Data
Names: Holbrook, Thomas M., author.
Title: Altered states : changing populations, changing parties, and the transformation of the
American political landscape / Thomas M. Holbrook.
Description: New York, NY : Oxford University Press, 2016. | Includes bibliographical
references and index.
Identifiers: LCCN 2015046541 | ISBN 9780190269128 (hardcover : alk. paper) |
ISBN 9780190269135 (pbk. : alk. paper)
Subjects: LCSH: Political culture—United States—States. | Demography—Political aspects—
United States—States. | Party affiliation—United States—States. | Voting—United States—States. |
Elections—United States—States. | Presidents—United States—Election.
Classification: LCC JK1726 .H648 2016 | DDC 324.0973—dc23 LC record available
at http://lccn.loc.gov/2015046541

9 8 7 6 5 4 3 2 1
Printed by Webcom, Inc., Canada

To Kathy, for everything, and to our children, Olivia and Clayton, who are terrific kids and make us proud.

CONTENTS

LIST OF FIGURES

LIST OF TABLES

ACKNOWLEDGMENTS

Everyone should have the good fortune to write a book about something in which they are truly interested. That is certainly the case with this book, which I had a lot of fun writing. It was challenging in many ways, but those challenges were themselves very rewarding.

I initially started thinking about some of the ideas in this book following the 2008 presidential election, motivated in part by Democratic victories in Florida, Indiana, North Carolina, and Virginia, states that are not usually considered part of the Democratic coalition. I originally assumed the reason for these Democratic victories was obvious: with the exception of Indiana, these were all states with large and growing black or Latino populations, so these outcomes must represent part of the "demographic problem" confronting the Republican Party. After looking more closely at outcomes for all states, across decades of elections, it was clear that something much broader in scope was going on: a number of other states had moved in the Democratic direction, and many of them didn't fit into the traditional race- and ethnicity-based "demography is destiny" framework as well as Florida, North Carolina, and Virginia did, and there were just as many states that had moved toward the Republican Party during the same time period. Clearly something was going on, and that something was not as simple as changes in the racial and ethnic makeup of the state populations. As it turned out, the "demography is destiny" framework is much more nuanced and reflects changes in multiple and varied population characteristics, many of which are connected to changes in party support in the states. Besides changes in population characteristics, it seemed clear that something else was going on. State populations were not the only elements that had changed over the previous several decades. Political parties had grown much more polarized at the elite level, and social group alignments with the parties had also changed appreciably and sometimes in nonobvious ways. The theoretical framework used here argues that these two types of changes—changes in state characteristics (compositional effects) and changes in how those characteristics are correlated with state outcomes (contextual effects)—may be responsible for the important geographic transformation of American presidential elections that has taken place in recent decades.

Writing this book was a fairly solitary process. That said, a number of people provided help along the way and had a significant impact on the final product. My first pass at this material was for a Midwest Political Science Association (MPSA) paper in 2014. The discussant on the panel, Vlad Kogan, not only provided comments at the meeting but also sent me more detailed written comments soon thereafter. It was while working on the MPSA paper that it first occurred to me the topic would lend itself better to a book than to a paper. The paper was way too long, and I was barely able to scratch the surface of what I wanted to do. But I needed time to think and time to write. I was able to use a one-semester sabbatical leave (spring 2015) but was really able to jumpstart things in the fall of 2014 with a teaching reduction I worked out with Associate Dean Jim Moyer and Dean Rodney Swain of the College of Letters and Science at University of Wisconsin at Milwaukee. Having that fall semester course reduction was critical for clearing the deck of other matters and putting together a prospectus for this book. Carisa Bergner provided important assistance with some of the initial data gathering when she was my research assistant. My colleague Dave Armstrong was a tremendous resource whenever I found myself stuck on methodological issues or unable to decide among multiple versions of the same graphic. Dave has good methodological intuition and a keen eye for data visualization, and I took full advantage of his willingness to help. My colleagues Hong Min Park and Ivan Ascher also provided input, and Aaron Weinschenk was generous enough to read and provide valuable feedback on the entire manuscript.

A number of other people provided help. Barry Burden and his colleagues at UW-Madison provided important feedback early in the process when I presented some of this material to the UW-Madison American Politics Workshop. Likewise Nate Birkhead, Brianne Heidbreder, and their colleagues at Kansas State University provided valuable input and hospitality when I made a presentation to their department. I need to single out Peter Enns for being particularly generous with his time. His willingness to provide multiple variations of the state party and ideology data from his project with Julianna Koch (Enns and Koch 2013) was tremendously helpful. Peter tolerated my unsolicited pestering and went well beyond the call of duty in sharing his data. I hope I put them to good use, and, of course, I bear sole responsibility for how they are used.

I am also appreciative of the growing coffee shop culture in Milwaukee for providing me with a number of satellite offices. It was nice to have somewhere to go other than my office in the attic, somewhere I could find a good cup of coffee and get a couple solid hours of work done. One has to balance quality of coffee and the quality of the work environment when choosing satellite offices, and I found the best combinations of both at Colectivo on Prospect Avenue, Stone Creek in Shorewood, and Starbucks on Downer Avenue. Much of the work for this book was done at these three places.

I'd also like to thank Angela Chnapko, my editor at Oxford University Press. The publication of this book was somewhat time-sensitive; I submitted my prospectus in November 2014 with the intention of the book coming out prior to the 2016 elections, so I needed to find a press where that seemed feasible. Angela got that from the beginning and agreed that it only made sense to push the book for publication prior to the election. She was quick to reply to my initial inquiries, getting my prospectus out to reviewers right away, and I ended up with a contract to sign within just a couple of months. The rest of the project has received similar attention and moved swiftly throughout the process. Princess Ikatekit and Jeyashree Ramamoorthy were also very helpful throughout the process.

I also benefited immensely from the anonymous reviewers at both the prospectus and final manuscript review stages. More than anything, the reviewer comments helped me better understand where this book fits in the broader literature on political change and suggested ways that I could clarify my argument and my findings. This is a much-improved book as a result of that input.

Finally I owe the most sincere debt of gratitude to Kathy Dolan, my wife, colleague, and partner. Kathy provided support on so many levels that it is hard to describe. Beyond being a thorough and willing proof-reader and providing advice along the way, Kathy was very supportive and encouraging, always looking for ways to facilitate my work on this project. This meant, even more so than usual, a lot of heavy lifting around the house and with the kids, and putting up with the occasional sour mood. For this and everything, thanks, Dear.

Altered States

The Changing Political Landscape

Many in the Republican Party leadership are concerned about their party's long-term prospects in U.S. presidential elections. The 2012 presidential election was the second consecutive defeat for the Republican Party and the fourth defeat out of the last six presidential elections. Though neither the 2008 nor 2012 election was particularly close in outcome, they were by no means lopsided losses and they could be explained, at least in part, by prevailing national conditions. In 2008 the Republican candidate, Senator John McCain from Arizona, was weighed down by almost unparalleled negative conditions as the incumbent party nominee: the financial collapse gained steam in the middle of September with the collapse of Lehman Brothers; the October 2008 unemployment rate (6.5%) had grown an alarming 1.8 points over the preceding twelve months; the third-quarter growth rate in real gross domestic product (GDP) was −1.9%; and President George W. Bush's approval rating in October 2008 averaged 26.5%.[1] In 2012 the Republican nominee, former Massachusetts governor Mitt Romney, ran under conditions that favored reelection for the Democratic incumbent, President Barak Obama: the October 2012 unemployment rate (7.8%), though higher than in 2008, had dropped a full point in one year; the third-quarter growth rate for GDP was 2.5%; and presidential approval averaged 50.8% in October. It is not difficult to argue that Senator McCain was in a fight he couldn't win and Governor Romney also was somewhat disadvantaged.

Some pundits and party activists take the results of these and other elections as a sign of trouble for the long-term prospects for Republican success in pursuit of the White House. In fact there is even some talk of an emerging and insurmountable Democratic Party advantage in the Electoral College. Republican strategists Mike Murphy and Trent Wisecup (2013) summed up this perspective: "The GOP's biggest challenge is the fact that the Democrats begin each presidential election with a near lock on the Electoral College." This could be viewed as a simple case of sour grapes from the losing side, but others without the same vested interest echo this notion: Nate Silver (2012) pointed out that Romney needed to do much better than pulling even in the popular vote to have had a shot at winning the Electoral College, and Jonathan Bernstein (2012) found that the same was true for McCain in 2008. Even in the wake of tremendous Republican successes in the 2014 midterm elections, Republican columnist Chris Ladd (2014) suggests that Republicans should keep their optimism for the 2016 presidential election in check, lamenting, "The biggest Republican victory in decades did not move the map. The Republican party's geographic and demographic isolation from the rest of American actually got worse." Ladd's primary concern is what he refers to as the "Blue Wall" of states—states that Democratic candidates can count on winning—including a number of formerly Republican or competitive states.

This perceived Democratic "lock" is a fairly new phenomenon, as it was not so long ago that Democrats bemoaned the "Republican lock" on the Electoral College and saw little hope for the future. In fact it is reported that Horace Busby, an aide to President Lyndon B. Johnson, was the first to use the term *electoral lock*, but to describe the Republican rather than the Democratic advantage in the Electoral College (Destler 1996). Talk of a current Democratic advantage also flies in the face of uneven population growth of the past several decades, during which traditionally Democratic regions (Upper Midwest and Northeast) grew at much slower rates than Republican-leaning regions (South and Southwest), a pattern typically seen as putting the Democrats into an increasingly tough political corner (Burmila 2009) as electoral votes swell in Republican areas.

How can it be that Republican states are growing at faster rates than Democratic states, but the Republican Party finds itself at an increasing Electoral College disadvantage? One possibility is that the Electoral College disadvantage is more imagined than real. This point is taken up later in this chapter, where the evidence shows that while there is hardly a Democratic lock on the Electoral College, the Democratic Party has improved its position in the Electoral College over time. Another explanation, in fact the one that gets the most attention, focuses not on the change in the number of people in Republican or Democratic states but on changes in the types of people living in those states. According to this account Republican states that have grown in population and electoral votes simply may not be as Republican as they once were, due in part to important demographic changes that have made electoral life more difficult for Republican presidential candidates. This idea echoes John Judis and Ruy Teixeira's (2004) sense over ten years ago of the impending problems that the changing American demographic profile would pose for the Republican Party. Most of the talk along these lines focuses on the increasing size of the minority vote, especially the Latino vote, and its concentration in key states. For instance, addressing the electoral impact of immigration policy, Rand Paul, the Republican senator from Kentucky, recently argued, "Texas is going to be a Democratic State within 10 years if we don't change" (Gluek 2014). This belief in the potential impact of demographic changes has even motivated Democratic leaders to mount a new effort (nicknamed Battleground Texas) aimed at converting Texas to a Democratic state by mobilizing Latino and black voters (Burns 2013). While Democrats' aspirations for Texas may outstrip their actual prospects, Democratic presidential candidates have made important advances in formerly Republican and competitive states, advances that have improved their position in the Electoral College.

EVIDENCE OF POLITICAL CHANGE

There are two related questions here, both of which are theoretically interesting and potentially very important to electoral politics. First, have there been changes in the relative strength of the Democratic and Republican parties in the Electoral College? There certainly has been political chatter to the effect that Republicans have moved from a position of superiority to one of vulnerability. But this is an empirical question and is best dealt with by a systematic assessment of national and state voting patterns. Second, have there been substantively important changes in the geographic basis of party support in presidential elections, changes that can be explained in theoretically interesting ways? While there has been some speculation about how the changing racial and ethnic profiles of some states have affected their political orientation, a broader view of changes in political support across all fifty states is needed, one that explores myriad other potential sources of change. These are important matters with significant implications for U.S. presidential elections, and it is essential to document the scope of the changes that have taken place before attempting to explain how those changes have come about. Although changes in Electoral College strength have clear consequences for the parties, shifting allegiances among the states also offer an important opportunity to test theories of political change, and it is this question that I focus on primarily throughout this book. Before proceeding to theoretical explanations of political change, however, we need to be clear about how much (if any) change has occurred and where that change has taken place.

The rest of this chapter is data rich, presenting mostly descriptive evidence of the magnitude, direction, and consequences of changes in party support in presidential outcomes in the states. The evidence shows that an important political transformation has occurred, a transformation reflected not just in Democratic victories at the national level but also, and more dramatically, a transformation of the geographic bases of Democratic and Republican success. Most of the analysis throughout this book utilizes presidential elections from 1972 to 2012 to gauge the magnitude and direction of political change in the states. This forty-year time frame provides rich variation in outcomes and encompasses important political changes within both parties: the Republican Party before, during, and after the Reagan Revolution, and the Democratic Party from the liberal candidacies of McGovern and Mondale to the New Democratic (centrists) candidacies of Clinton and Gore, to Obama as the first nonwhite major party nominee and president of the United States. Beginning the analysis in 1972 puts us on this side of the tumultuous events of the 1960s and the initial wave of partisan changes connected to shifting party positions on civil rights (Carmines and Stimson 1989), while still placing us more squarely in the modern party era and prior to changes in the parties that occurred in the 1980s, 1990s, and 2000s.[2]

CHANGING NATIONAL POWER

Although my primary interest is in changes among the states over time, it is the impact of those changes on national outcomes that is important to the parties and is the basis of many Republican concerns. Shifting patterns of party support in the states would be of much less concern to party leaders if the net effect of those changes had little impact on national outcomes. Analyzing changes in national party strength provides a context for evaluating changes in the states, and linking those changes to the Electoral College highlights their importance. The data presented in Figure 1.1 illustrate changes in party fortunes at the national level, focusing on the Republican electoral vote count (solid line) and the Republican share of the popular vote (dashed line) over time. Using these outcomes as the basis for judging party prospects, it is easy to see why Republican leaders are dismayed. Indeed the pattern in this figure appears to depict two different eras: one of relative Republican dominance (1972–88) and one of increased parity, if not a slight Democratic advantage (1992–2012). With the single exception of 1976—an election in which the Republican candidate Gerald Ford barely lost to the Democrat Jimmy Carter—the Republican Party dominated presidential elections in the early period. And the loss in 1976 could be explained by circumstances that were unique to that election cycle: post-Watergate reaction to the Republican Party and Carter's unique appeal to southern voters, who previously had been abandoning the Democratic Party in the wake of its support for civil rights (Carmines and Stimson 1989). The later period is hardly a complete reversal of fortunes, since the Democrats do not enjoy the same level of dominance, but it clearly represents a period of decline for the

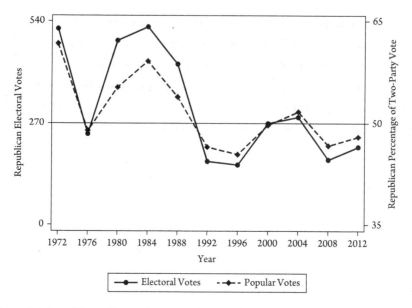

Figure 1.1 Republican Electoral Votes and Share of the Two-Party Popular Vote, 1972–2012

Republicans: from 1992 to 2012 Republican presidential candidates won the Electoral College only twice, and one of those times was the disputed outcome of 2000, in which their victory came down to confusing ballots and recount politics (Imai and King 2004; Wand et al. 2001).

As much as the Electoral College is what ultimately matters the most, it should also be disconcerting for Republican leaders that their candidates lost the national popular vote in five of six elections from 1992 to 2012. This highlights one important explanation for the Republican Party's Electoral College "problem": its popular vote problem. One could look at Figure 1.1 and conclude that there is no Electoral College mystery to be solved, that all the Republican Party needs to do to win more electoral votes is win a greater share of the popular vote. But it is not quite that simple. The real question is not whether Republicans have lost standing in the popular vote but rather whether the electoral vote "return" on their popular vote share has declined.

One way to get a better handle on this issue is to estimate how many electoral votes Republican candidates could expect to receive under different popular vote scenarios in each election and then determine whether there has been any decline in the expected electoral vote distribution associated with those scenarios over time. Given that the Electoral College outcome is most in doubt in relatively close election cycles, the scenarios used here are toss-up and very close national popular vote outcomes. In the data series in Figure 1.1 there are only two outcomes that can be considered very close or toss-ups (1976, 2000), so we don't have many "real" outcomes on which to base any conclusion. Instead we can look at each election in this series and estimate how many electoral votes the parties would have won if the popular vote outcome had been a toss-up (Republican candidate 50%) or a very close outcome (Republican candidate getting 49 or 51%). To do this the Republican candidate's actual share of the two-party vote in each state is expressed as a deviation from the Republican share of the national two-party vote in each year and then added to the simulated Republican national vote shares (49, 50, and 51% of two-party vote). Consider a couple of states from the 2012 election, a year in which the Republican candidate, Romney, garnered 48% of the national two-party vote. In 2012 Romney took 49.56% of the two-party vote in Florida (1.56 points higher than his national vote share) and 47.27% of the two-party vote in Pennsylvania (.73 points lower than his national vote share). If we assume for the sake of simulating outcomes that states maintain their relative position vis-à-vis the national vote (admittedly a somewhat sketchier assumption in years with landslide victories), then we can estimate that Romney would have carried Florida with approximately 51.56% and lost Pennsylvania with approximately 49.27% of the two-party vote if the national popular vote outcome had been 50/50. Likewise if he had garnered 49% of the national two-party vote, Romney still would have won Florida and lost Pennsylvania, and he would have won both states if he had received 51% of the national two-party vote.[3]

This same technique is used in Figure 1.2 to estimate hypothetical outcomes for all states from 1972 to 2012 and document trends in party advantage in the Electoral College. Here we have three different lines representing the expected Republican electoral votes in scenarios where they win 49, 50, and 51% of the national popular vote. The elections are grouped together to smooth out some of the bumpiness that occurs due to idiosyncrasies of

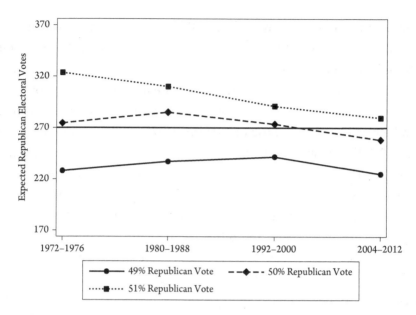

Figure 1.2 Expected Republican Electoral Votes under Alternative Popular Vote Scenarios

NOTE: The estimated Republican electoral votes are calculated by taking the Republican candidate's actual share of the two-party vote in each state, expressing it as a deviation from the Republican candidate's share of the national two-party vote in each year, and then adding the hypothetical Republican national vote shares (49, 50, and 51% of two-party vote). The electoral votes the Republican candidate would have won under these scenarios are then summed to get the total expected electoral vote count. Each data point represents the average expected electoral votes for that time period.

single election cycles, in particular the effects of home state and regional (southern effect for the Carter and Clinton candidacies) advantages.[4] Let's focus, first, on scenarios in which the vote is a toss-up, split 50/50. In such circumstances the expected Electoral College outcomes tilt slightly in the Republican direction in the 1970s, 1980s, and 1990s. However, from 2004 to 2012 toss-up popular votes would have favored the Democratic Party. Of course in all of the toss-up scenarios, the estimated electoral vote margin is very narrow, but the Republicans' edge is greatest in the 1980s, when their estimated electoral vote count was, on average, 280, a number later matched by an expected Democratic count of 280 in the 2004–12 period. A more dramatic decline in Republican strength is found in the scenario in which the Republican candidate wins 51% of the two-party popular vote: after averaging 324 expected electoral votes in the 1970s Republicans average just 280 expected electoral votes in 2004–12. This represents an impressive decline in electoral vote security, moving steadily from a relatively safe and substantial margin to a narrow margin that could be lost with the movement of just one or two states. Finally, there is not a clear pattern in the scenario in which the Republican candidate garners 49% of the two-party vote, but it is notable that the expected electoral vote count is at its lowest point (just barely) in the 2004–12 period.

There are two main takeaway points from Figure 1.2. First, Republican woes in the Electoral College are not due just to poor performance in the popular vote, though their lives would be made easier if they increased their vote share. Certainly both parties are relatively certain to win the Electoral College vote if they take a substantial majority of the two-party vote, and the Republican Party would probably eek out a victory with 51%. The problem for the Republican Party is that it has lost the advantage it once held in narrow popular vote outcomes. Under different popular vote scenarios, there is clear evidence that the Republican Electoral College return on popular votes has declined over time: where Democrats used to be disadvantaged in toss-up elections, Republicans are now disadvantaged, and where a narrow lead in the popular vote once was associated with a substantial Electoral College advantage for Republicans, it now gives them only a narrow margin. The second point is that this doesn't mean the sky is falling for Republicans, nor that Democrats have anything resembling a lock on the Electoral College. To be sure, there has been something of a role reversal, such that Democrats might be slightly advantaged, but that advantage is not insurmountable. Still something is afoot, something that suggests a changing dynamic and requires further explanation.

CHANGES AMONG THE STATES

One suspect in the case of diminishing Republican success is the changing geographic pattern of support for the parties. However, a number of conditions should be met in order for shifting state allegiances to serve as an interesting explanation for the increased Democratic edge in the

Electoral College. First, there needs to have been substantial and substantively interesting changes over time in party support across the fifty states. Among other things, this means there needs to have been change in more than just one, two, or a few states. However, change across multiple states is not enough, as it is possible that states could change in offsetting ways that have little effect on the overall Electoral College picture. If this were the case, the changes among states would still be interesting and worth studying, but it would be more difficult to tie them to changes in party power. So, second, it is also necessary that the changes among the states, on balance, favor the Democratic Party—that Democrats have gained strength in states that account for more electoral votes than those states in which Republicans have gained strength. Third, there should be heterogeneity in the pattern of change across the states rather than something like a uniform shift across the states. A uniform shift across states could certainly explain changes in the Electoral College, but it wouldn't provide a very interesting context for evaluating changes in state outcomes. As it happens, the data used here meet all of these conditions.

The key to measuring political change in the states is capturing the trends in political support over time, separately, for each of the fifty states, while also being able to organize and interpret the fifty separate trends in a way that sheds light on the net impact of those changes. As a first step in assessing change, I estimate the centered (around the national vote division) Democratic share of the two-party vote separately for each state in each year (1972 to 2012). Centering the vote on the national two-party division in the popular vote permits a comparison across states without having to also consider factors (national political tides) that affect the overall level of party support from one year to the next. Centering also places the emphasis not on which party wins or loses a state in a given year but on support for the Democratic Party over time in a given state *relative* to all other states.[5]

To gauge the trend over time I used ordinary least squares (OLS) regression and regress centered vote share on year, separately for each state, and also included dummy variables for presidential and vice-presidential home state advantage, as well as one for southern states in 1976 and 1980, and in 1992 and 1996. The southern dummy variable is necessary to capture the unnaturally high level of support for the Democratic ticket in the

South in response to the candidacies of Georgia governor Jimmy Carter, and Arkansas governor Bill Clinton.[6] The results from the state-by-state regression models are then used to estimate the state-by-state trends in Democratic support over time. This is done by setting the values for the home state and regional dummy variables to zero so the "predictions" reflect the trend over time exclusive of these transitory perturbations.

Figures 1.3 and 1.4 document the changes in Democratic fortunes across the fifty states.[7] In each figure the solid straight line represents the estimated trend in Democratic support over time, and the points represent

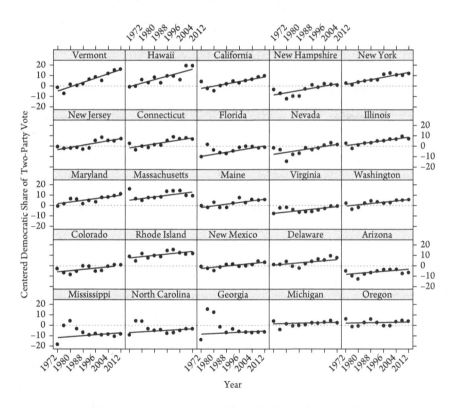

Figure 1.3 Trends in Party Support in Presidential Elections among Twenty-Five States with Greatest Democratic Gains, 1972–2012

NOTE: Each of the dots represents a centered state election outcome—specifically the Democratic percentage of the two-party vote in the state minus the Democratic percentage of the national two-party vote. The lines in each scatter plot summarize the linear trend in the election outcomes over time, controlling for presidential and vice-presidential home state advantage and a southern regional effect in the 1976–80 and 1992–96 elections.

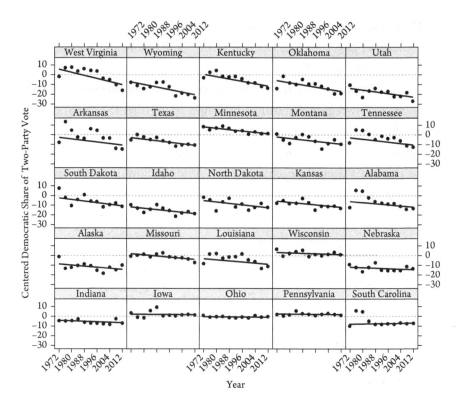

Figure 1.4 Trends in Party Support in Presidential Elections among Twenty-Five States with Greatest Democratic Losses, 1972–2012

NOTE: Each of the dots represents a centered state election outcome—specifically the Democratic percentage of the two-party vote in the state minus the Democratic percentage of the national two-party vote. The lines in each scatter plot summarize the linear trend in the election outcomes over time, controlling for presidential and vice-presidential home state advantage and a southern regional effect in the 1976–80 and 1992–96 elections.

the actual election outcomes. It is important to recall that in some cases the trend line does not appear to fit the scatter plot as well as it should because it excludes the effects of home state and regional advantages (see North Carolina, Mississippi, and Georgia in 1976 and 1980 as examples of this phenomenon). These deviations illustrate the importance of controlling for regional and home state effect in order to ascertain something resembling the normal level of party support in the states. It is also worth pointing out that the observations above the zero point (dashed line) are not necessarily cases in which the Democratic candidate won the state;

instead these are cases in which the Democratic candidate fared better than his national two-party vote share. Consider Minnesota in 1972, one of the forty-nine states lost by the Democratic nominee, South Dakota senator George McGovern (see Figure 1.4). Despite this loss, Minnesota was still a *relatively* strong Democratic state in 1972, since McGovern ran about 9 points better there than his national vote share. Centering the state outcome on the two-party national vote places Minnesota in context and shows it to be a strong Democratic state in 1972 relative to other states and the national tide.

Figure 1.3 displays the pattern of partisan change among those twenty-five states in which the Democrats made their greatest gains, ordered by magnitude of gains from upper left (across rows) to lower right. The range in magnitude of change is vast, encompassing states like Vermont and Hawaii, where Democrats gained 14 and 16 points, respectively, to states like Michigan and Oregon, where the Democratic gain is so slight (about 1 point) that it is barely visible. Magnitude of change is not the only consideration, however. Instead, in order to fully comprehend the potential importance of change, it is critical to consider both magnitude of change and where the states stood to begin with. Using these criteria, these states generally fall into several different categories. There are states that had been somewhat competitive and then favored the Democratic candidate: California, Connecticut, Delaware, Hawaii, Illinois, Maine, Maryland, New Jersey, New Mexico (very slightly), New York, Vermont, and Washington. Some of these states leaned slightly Democratic or Republican in the early 1970s while others were truly toss-up states, but almost all of them have moved comfortably into the Democratic column.

Another important group consists of those states that had tilted Republican but became quite competitive: Colorado, Florida, New Hampshire, Nevada, and Virginia. In addition, while North Carolina is not quite as competitive as the others, it has been drifting competitive over time. To be sure, these are not states that the Democratic candidate can count on—they are, after all, competitive—but they used to be farther out of reach for the Democrats and now are up for grabs. There also are states that had been strongly Democratic and became even more so

(Massachusetts and Rhode Island) and several states where the change was either very slight and didn't alter the general outlook for either party (Arizona, Georgia, and Mississippi) or that can best be described as flatliners, impervious to whatever process has driven the changes in other states (the already mentioned Michigan and Oregon). Technically there has been some change in this last group of states, but it is so slight that it is barely discernible in these plots.

Of course not all states have trended so favorably toward the Democrats. The panel of graphs in Figure 1.4 illustrates the pattern of party change in the remaining states, where Democrats either lost ground to Republicans or just managed to hold their own. One state that stands out here is West Virginia, which has shifted from being a place where the Democratic candidate typically ran ahead of the national vote to a place that now appears to be a long shot for Democratic candidates. Minnesota is another interesting state. Although Democratic candidates continue to fare slightly better in Minnesota than in the nation as a whole, there has been a very gradual decline in that advantage: Democrats went from running about 8 points higher than the national vote in the first three elections in this series to an average of just over 2 points above the national vote in the past three elections. Democrats continue to outperform the national vote there, but by a much smaller margin. Although the change is much less dramatic, Republicans have made slight gains in Wisconsin. While the Badger State has sided with every Democratic presidential candidate since 1988, Democrats have outperformed their national vote share there by only a couple of points, on average, in the past few election cycles.

Probably the most consequential states in Figure 1.4 are those that had been somewhat competitive (mostly slightly Republican) but then grew to clearly favor the Republican candidate: Arkansas, Kentucky, Louisiana, Missouri, Montana, South Dakota, Tennessee, and Texas. (So much for the Democratic project Battleground Texas.) In strong Democratic years these states were once possible pickups for the Democrats, but they now appear to be out of reach. Of course a number of states were already fairly Republican in the early 1970s and have become even more so over time: Alabama, Alaska, Idaho, Kansas, North Dakota, Oklahoma, Utah, and Wyoming. And there is also another group of flat-liners, displaying very little change: Indiana, Iowa, Ohio, Nebraska, Pennsylvania, and South Carolina.

Figures 1.3 and 1.4 show that political change in the states has been a varied experience, in which both parties have gained strength in some states while growing weaker in others, and in which some states show clear trends while others have barely moved over the past forty years. These are exactly the types of patterns that cry out for clarification and explanation. These trends can be further condensed to help provide a clearer picture of the magnitude of the changes that have occurred, as well as their net effect on party fortunes. Figure 1.5 captures both the direction and the magnitude of changes in party support in state-level presidential elections. In this figure the arrows pointing to the left identify states in which the trend has favored Republican presidential candidates, and the arrows pointing to the right identify those states in which Democrats have made gains. The blunt end of the arrow represents the starting point—the state average during the 1972–80 elections—and the point at the head of the arrow designates where the states end up, on average, for presidential elections in 2004–12. These beginning and end points are based on the estimated levels of support from the separate state slopes in Figures 1.3 and 1.4. It is important to recall that party support is expressed relative to the Democratic share of the national presidential vote in each year. One advantage of centering on the national vote is that the zero point is more easily interpreted in terms of level of competition. If the national vote outcome is split 50/50, then the zero point indicates that the expected state outcome would also be 50/50, values greater than zero indicate a Democratic victory, and values less than zero indicate a Republican victory. As the arrows move away from the midpoint in either direction, outcomes are less competitive.

Figure 1.5 reinforces a couple of points that were somewhat more difficult to glean from the scatter plots. First, there is a lot of movement in both directions, and both the magnitude and the direction of change vary appreciably across states. This is important from an analytical perspective: in explaining political change, the interest is in accounting not just

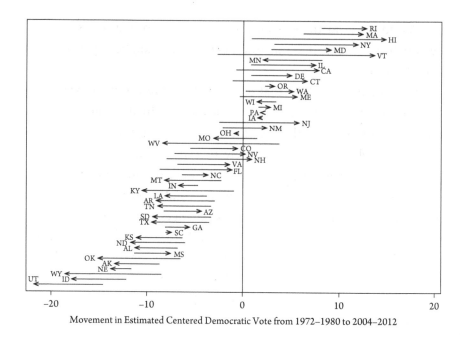

Movement in Estimated Centered Democratic Vote from 1972–1980 to 2004–2012

Figure 1.5 The Magnitude and Direction of Change in Party Support in Presidential Elections, 1972–80 to 2004–12

NOTE: The arrows pointing to the left identify states where Republican presidential candidates made gains from 1972 to 2012, and the arrows pointing to the right identify states in which Democrats have made gains. The difference between these beginning and end points reflects the movement in party support during this time period and is based on the estimated levels of support from the separate state slopes in Figures 1.3 and 1.4. The blunt end of the arrow represents the estimated state average during the 1972–80 elections, and the tip of the arrow represents the estimated state average for presidential elections in 2004–12.

for Democratic growth but also Republican growth, as well as cases in which states did not move much at all. All of these patterns play a role in shaping party strength. Another pattern that is made somewhat clearer here is that Democratic and Republican increases come from different sources. Overall, states in which Republicans gained strength tend to be those in which they already had an advantage in the popular vote. Fully 75% of Republican gains (regardless of magnitude) occurred in states in which Republican candidates already had an edge. This *consolidation* pattern stands in stark contrast to the pattern for the Democratic Party of both consolidation and *penetration*: only 38% of Democratic gains occurred in states where Democrats already held an edge in the 1970s, with the remaining gains coming in states where Republicans previously held an edge. While the Republican pattern of consolidation has the potential benefit of making more states a sure thing for the Republican Party, it also results in important overall net gains for the Democrats, as there are fewer instances of Republican inroads in Democratic states.

In very broad terms there is a clear trend in favor of Democratic presidential candidates. Looking just at the direction of movement (ignoring magnitude), the parties are fairly even in terms of the number of states where they post gains: twenty-six states for Democrats and twenty-four for Republicans. However, there is a substantial difference in the number of electoral votes associated with the two groups of states: the states where Democrats made inroads control 322 electoral votes, while the states with Republican gains control just 213 electoral votes. This is a large and meaningful difference, but it may misrepresent the case somewhat for a number of reasons: some states in which the parties gained strength were already in the Democratic or Republican column and only became more strongly partisan (more so for Republicans); in a few states where a party gained strength (e.g., Mississippi and Georgia for the Democrats, and Minnesota and Wisconsin for the Republicans), their position is improved but they are still at a disadvantage; and there are a handful of states where movement was very slight, hardly representing real change in status, though on balance in one party's favor.

These issues can be addressed by focusing on cases of conversion (switching from one party to another) and changes in states' competitive status (moving from competitive to noncompetitive or from noncompetitive to competitive). Figure 1.6 highlights the twenty-two states that fall into either of these categories. The vertical lines are –2 and +2 percentage points, representing a band of competitive outcomes. There is only one state (West Virginia) that can be described as clearly switching from solidly one party (Democratic) to the other (Republican), while the remaining twenty-one states moved into or out of the competitive zone. Vermont also comes close to a conversion, though I would describe it as moving from leaning Republican to solid Democrat. Across all twenty-two states whose competitive status changed, only six states, representing 59

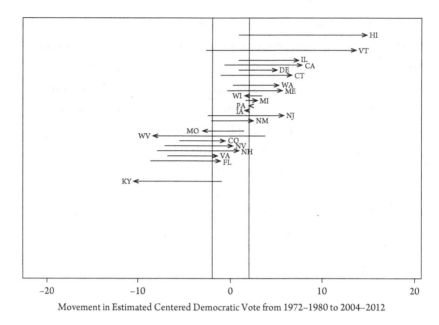

Movement in Estimated Centered Democratic Vote from 1972–1980 to 2004–2012

Figure 1.6 The Magnitude and Direction of Change in Party Support in Presidential Elections among States That Experienced Change in Their Competitive Status

NOTE: This figure is limited to those states that experienced a change in their competitive status—moving from one party to another, from competitive to favoring one party, or from one party to competitive—between 1972–80 and 2004–12. See Figure 1.6 for an explanation of the contents.

electoral votes, moved in the Republican direction, while sixteen states, representing 209 electoral votes, moved in the Democratic direction. This is a decidedly lopsided change in favor of Democratic candidates and no doubt contributes to changes in party performance in the Electoral College discussed earlier, changes that have improved the position of the Democratic Party, albeit short of giving them a lock.

There are also important regional patterns of change. These patterns are captured in Figure 1.7, which uses the beginning and end points of the arrows in Figure 1.5 to represent the average level of centered party support in 1972–80 and 2004–12, respectively. Here the lighter shades indicate greater Republican strength, and darker shades indicate greater Democratic strength. Although the trends are not perfectly consistent, there are clear regional patterns to changes in party support. West Coast, southwestern, northeastern, and mid-Atlantic states (and Florida) are

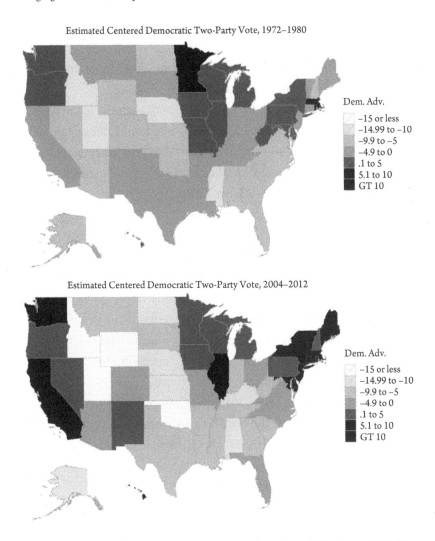

Figure 1.7 Geographic Changes in Party Support in Presidential Elections, 1972–80 to 2004–12

NOTE: Estimated centered Democratic share of the two-party vote is based on the average estimated values of centered Democratic vote, based on the slopes presented in Figures 1.3 and 1.4, for each time period. Maps were generated using Choroplethr.

appreciably darker, and more Democratic, in the bottom (2004–12) map than in the top (1972–80) map, and the shading of the Plains, Mountain West, border, and Deep South states has grown much lighter, indicating growth in Republican power. The changes in the Plains and Mountain West states are emblematic of the pattern of Republican consolidation noted earlier. The entire column of states from North Dakota to Texas, as well as most (but not all) of the Mountain West, were already in the Republican camp (light in tone), by varying degrees, in the 1970s and became even more strongly Republican by the 2000s.

Overall the patterns of change are consistent with the idea that some of the changes in Republican strength in the Electoral College can be tied to changes in the political alignment of the states. First, there have been substantial changes in state political allegiances over time, and these changes represent more than just a uniform shift across the fifty states. A number of states have grown more supportive of the Democratic Party, a number have moved toward the Republican Party, and still other states have not moved much at all. Two important characteristics of state political change point to net Democratic gains: the number of electoral votes represented by states that moved Democratic far exceeds those represented by states that moved Republican, and Republican gains were much more likely to come in states where Republicans already had an advantage over Democrats, while Democratic gains were more likely to represent inroads into formerly competitive or Republican states. These patterns certainly could be responsible for changes in Republican Electoral College performance. Setting that connection aside, though, the breadth and scope of the changes represent an important opportunity to learn about the process of political change.

RELATED ISSUES

Before analyzing the roots of political change, I take a brief look at two related issues: the extent to which the findings for presidential elections reflect broader changes in elections at other levels of government, and the extent to which the patterns presented here reflect a trend toward increased geographic polarization.

Political Change in Other Elections?

The data presented thus far illustrate important changes in the geographic bases of support for parties and presidential elections. These changes, and several alternative potential explanations for them, are the primary focus of this book. Nevertheless one important consideration is the extent to which the changes in political support shown here extend more broadly to other levels of elected office. On one hand, it is reasonable to expect that the forces that produced the changes noted here should have effects that extend beyond the presidential level. After all, the dynamics of group connections are about groups and parties, and the same two parties participate at all levels of government. On the other hand, the American party system, while dominated by two national parties, is decentralized to such a degree that the meaning of those parties and the nature of candidates vary a great deal from state to state. Presidential politics is about national politics and the national political parties, while state-level and even congressional elections are likely to have a much more local flavor. The Democratic Party in Nebraska and West Virginia is much more conservative than the national Democratic Party and can elect senators such as Ben Nelson (NE) and Joe Manchin (WV), who run appreciably to the right of the national party to suit local preferences. Likewise the Republican Party in Maine and Massachusetts is more liberal than the national Republican Party and can elect senators such as Olympia Snowe (ME), Susan Collins (ME), and Scott Brown (MA), who run appreciably to the left of the national party, also more aligned with local tastes. And of course candidates for governor, the state legislature, and local office have even more flexibility to appeal to local preferences, even if those preferences are out of sync with the national party. Presidential nominees don't have the same flexibility and can't run significantly to the right of their party in conservative states or to the left in liberal states, so it would not be surprising to find a much stronger pattern at the presidential level than at other levels of office.

Another factor that may create different patterns of partisan change across levels of government has to do with the power of incumbency, which is much stronger in congressional (Jacobson 2012), state-level (Hogan 2004; King 2001), and even local elections (Holbrook and Weinschenk 2014; Krebs 1998) than in presidential elections. Political change may happen more slowly where incumbency insulates officeholders from secular trends, and even against the effects of strong, short-term national tides. So, for instance, southern states that had long since moved toward the Republican Party at the presidential level took much longer to embrace Republican candidates at lower levels of office due in part to incumbency, but also because southern Democratic congressional and state-level candidates were typically much closer to local ideological leanings than to the ideological leanings of the national Democratic Party (Black and Black 2009).

Despite these impediments to change, it still makes sense to expect, over the long haul, that states that have trended Democratic or Republican at the presidential level should also do so at lower levels of office. This is not to say we should expect trends that are as pronounced as those found in presidential elections. In fact the expectation is that the trends will be somewhat more muted. I use state legislative elections to get a sense of the universality of the trends in party support identified earlier.[8] Specifically I focus on changes in the Democratic proportion of seats in the lower and upper houses of the state legislature. As was the case with presidential returns, it is important to center the Democratic share of seats on the national average. In this case, however, it is important to do so not just because of substantial swings from one election cycle to the next but also because of the long-term, secular trend in Democratic losses in state legislatures. This trend is due almost solely to Democratic losses in the South. In the early 1970s, when southern states were ready to move on and distance themselves from the Democratic Party in presidential elections, Democrats still averaged upward of 80% of all state legislative seats in southern states; this rate declined steadily until it finally dropped below 50% in the 2010s. In the rest of the country there is no clear trend in Democratic state legislative seats, though there is some bouncing around, particularly in response to national tides. In fact from 1972 to 2012 the correlation between time (year) and Democratic share of state house and state senate seats is –.11 for both chambers in states outside the South, and –.72 and –.74, respectively, for southern states. Given this regional difference, it is also important to examine the connection between presidential and state legislative trends separately for southern and nonsouthern states.

To assess the correspondence between presidential and state legislative trends, I first estimated the trend in Democratic support over time separately for each of forty-nine states (Nebraska is excluded because it uses a nonpartisan state legislature), following roughly the same procedure used to generate Figures 1.3 and 1.4, except there were no short-term dummy variables to control for transitory effects, such as home state and home region. An OLS regression line was estimated using year as the independent variable and Democratic share of state legislative seats, separately for each chamber, as the dependent variable. The slope of the regression line is used as the estimate of the extent of Democratic growth or decline in the states, just as the slopes from Figures 1.3 and 1.4 are used to estimate the growth or decline in Democratic strength in presidential elections. The slopes for presidential and state legislative elections are then correlated to get a sense of the extent to which state legislatures have followed the trend in presidential support over time. Across all forty-nine states there is a moderate, positive relationship: the correlation with the trend in presidential contests is .41 for lower houses and .42 for upper houses of the state legislatures. This somewhat modest relationship, however, ignores very important regional differences in trends in party support.

Figure 1.8 shows the relationship between the presidential and state legislative trends for both the upper and lower houses of the state legislature, separately for southern and nonsouthern states. In nonsouthern states there is a much stronger correlation between centered Democratic strength in the state legislature and centered support for Democratic presidential candidates, producing a correlation of .70 for lower houses and .62 for upper houses. In other words, outside the South Democrats have generally tended to improve their relative standing in state legislatures in states where they have also made gains at the presidential level. Southern states, on the other hand, present a completely different pattern: the correlation between the trend in Democratic strength in southern state legislatures and the trend in presidential elections is –.64 in the lower houses and –.50 in the upper houses.

These relatively strong negative correlations are mostly a function of differences between three states that stand out a bit—Kentucky,

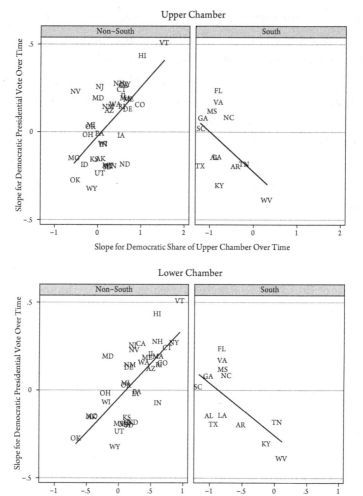

Figure 1.8 The Relationship between Changes in Democratic Strength in Presidential and State Legislative Elections, Controlling for the South

NOTE: The slopes for Democratic presidential vote over time are the estimates used to generate the slopes in Figures 1.3 and 1.4. The slopes for Democratic share of the legislative chambers are estimated in the same manner as the presidential slopes but using the Democratic share of the legislative chamber (centered around the national average) as the dependent variable.

Tennessee, and West Virginia—and the rest of the southern states. These three all grew substantially more Republican than the other states in presidential elections but saw smaller declines in relative Democratic power in state legislatures. The remaining southern states have experienced substantial declines in Democratic strength in their state legislatures but had a much more heterogeneous experience with presidential elections, ranging from substantial Democratic gains to somewhat more modest Democratic losses. One part of the explanation for the pattern among southern states relates to the overwhelming scope of Democratic control of some southern state governments in the early 1970s. In Kentucky, Tennessee, and West Virginia Democrats controlled roughly 65% of all state legislative seats, whereas in the remaining southern states they controlled roughly 90%. Borrowing from some of the work on congressional elections (Oppenheimer et al. 1986), Democrats were considerably overexposed in the most of the South and were more likely to see substantial losses there as the aftershocks of party changes in civil rights policy and the Republican alignment with the Christian Right worked their way through the electorate (Bishop 2009; Black and Black 2009; Carmines and Stimson 1989). At the same time, Democrats had already lost appreciable ground in presidential elections in the South by the early 1970s (setting aside the Carter candidacies) but still maintained some strength in Kentucky, Tennessee, and West Virginia and had farther to fall there. Given this context, the peculiar pattern in the South makes some sense. Outside the complicated politics of the South, however, the trends in relative support identified in presidential contests are similar to those found for state legislative contests.

Geographic Polarization?

Political polarization is an increasingly salient concept in the social sciences and plays an important role later in this book.[9] Typically polarization is conceived as significant attitudinal or political differences between Democrats and Republicans, or between social and demographic groups with partisan connections (Abramowitz 2010; Abramowitz and Saunders 2008; Fiorina et al. 2004). As Fiorina et al. so aptly point out, the level of polarization at the national level can be hard to uncover based just on the national popular vote division, since close election outcomes could be produced from vote distributions that are clear examples of either polarization or consensus. Similarly any given mean state outcome could be produced by either a polarized or a consensus distribution, so it is important to focus on the distribution of all state outcomes with an eye toward discerning polarized or consensus distributions. A typical consensus outcome would manifest itself in a distribution in which the states are tightly clustered around a central outcome, somewhere near the national outcome, with relatively few states occupying space on the extremes of the distribution. Whether there is a Democratic or a Republican winner, a landslide or a narrow outcome, in consensus elections most states don't stray far from the national outcome, and the shape of the distribution should look something like a bell-shaped curve. In contrast, polarization among the states would produce a distribution in which there is a tendency for states to be clustered at the high levels of relative Democratic or Republican support— at the tails of the distribution—with few states in the middle, reflecting something like Abramowitz's (2010) idea of a "disappearing center." The key point to the polarized distribution is that states tend to be heavily committed to one side or the other. There are very few closely contested outcomes, reminiscent of the pattern of "vanishing marginals" witnessed in congressional elections (Mayhew 1974), though in that case incumbency rather than polarization seems to have been the culprit. Most of the data presented in this chapter give the impression of an increasing gulf between Democratic and Republican states. For instance, in Figures 1.5 and 1.6 there appears to be a pattern of movement away from the center, with arrows pointing more toward the outside of the figure than to the middle. However, it is a bit difficult to divine levels and trends in polarization from the way the data have been presented so far.

A better sense of the distributional trend can be gleaned by examining the distribution of actual state outcomes separately for each year, using the descriptions of consensus and polarization outcomes provided above as referents. The graphs in Figure 1.9 utilize histograms (the chunky vertical bars) and kernel density plots (the lines used to smooth out the pattern in the histograms) to illustrate changes in the distribution of state votes over time. As with the preceding analyses, the state vote is centered on the national vote. Here it is easier to assess changes in polarization of state results. Although there is no dominant, consistent trend in the

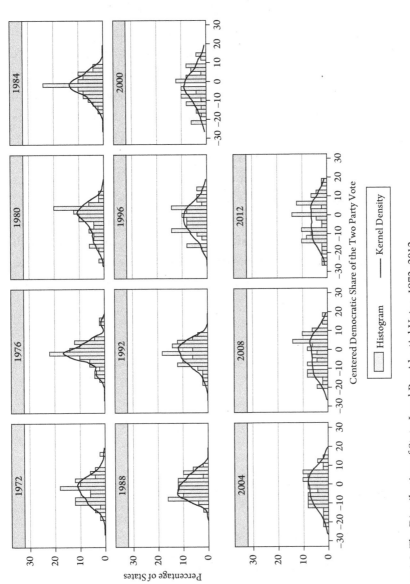

Figure 1.9 The Distribution of State-Level Presidential Votes, 1972–2012

NOTE: Histogram and kernel density plot both use the centered Democratic share of the two-party vote in the fifty states.

shape of the distributions, there was a tendency for elections in the 1970s, 1980s, and more or less in the 1990s to have a single-peak central tendency around which most of the states tended to cluster, resembling consensus more than polarization. The trend from 2000 to 2012 is for the vote to be much more dispersed, with less clustering in the middle. Two useful statistics—standard deviation and kurtosis—can be used to move beyond eyeballing the data and facilitate a bit more systematic assessment of the pattern. The standard deviation summarizes how much the data are spread out around the mean outcomes, with relatively high values indicating greater dispersion around the mean. By this measure (summarized with the solid line and left axis in Figure 1.10), state votes were more tightly clustered around the mean outcome in 1988 than in any other year, were more dispersed in 2012 than in any other year, and there was a general trend toward increased variation over time. Kurtosis is a statistic that is used to evaluate the peakness or flatness of a distribution, with positive numbers indicating a more distinct peak to the data and negative numbers indicate a flat or bimodal distribution. The kurtosis statistics

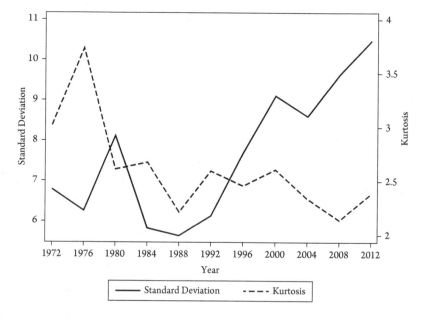

Figure 1.10 The Trend in Standard Deviation and Kurtosis for State-Level Centered Two-Party Presidential Votes, 1972–2012

(summarized with the dashed line and right axis in Figure 1.10) tell us that the distribution in 1976 was the clearest case of a peaked distribution and that 2008 was the least peaked distribution, and although it bounces around a bit, there is a downward trend in peakness over time. However, while the kurtosis values trend downward, they still are all positive values and hence do not suggest the flat or bimodal distributions one might expect to find with a polarized electorate. So while there is a trend *toward* flatter distributions, this is not a picture of a highly polarized electorate. Instead this is an electorate with an increasing tendency toward heterogeneity among the states, with more states clearly favoring one party over the other and fewer states occupying the middle ground. Highly polarized? No. Decreasing consensus? Yes.[10]

SUMMARY

There has been an interesting transformation of geographic bases of party support in presidential elections, a transformation that has consequences not just for the states that are in flux but also for the relative success of the parties at the national level. While on balance these changes have clearly benefited the Democratic Party, not all change has been in one direction: a process (or processes) is under way that has pushed some states toward the Democratic Party and others toward the Republican Party and has had relatively little effect on several states that have barely budged over the past forty years. Similar though much weaker and somewhat more complicated patterns of partisan change also occurred in state legislative elections, and there also is greater dispersion in state presidential outcomes as time goes on. At the same time these changes were taking place among the states, the Republican Party was also losing an edge it had in the Electoral College. Neither party has—or has had—anything resembling a lock on the Electoral College, but what was once a slight Republican advantage has been transformed into a slight Democratic edge.

My next task is to theorize about the processes that could account for the patterns of change among the states and then see how well those ideas empirically account for the changes that have taken place. The next

chapter provides an argument for the processes that might account for
state-level changes and summarizes what we have learned from existing
research. Briefly, the primary focus of the analysis is on two different types
of explanations: a compositional model (changes in the types of people
who live in a state) and a contextual model (changes in how much population characteristics matter at different points in time). The bulk of the rest
of the book provides the empirical tests of the models. Chapter 3 takes a
close look at how migration patterns influence changes in state outcomes,
in part by influencing changes in state population characteristics. The
migration analysis addresses the effects of both internal (state-to-state)
and external (foreign) migration. The treatment of internal migration is
a departure from most studies in that it focuses not just on the magnitude of internal migration among the states but also on the impact of the
political environment of the states in which internal migrants were born.
The idea is that there is no single expectation that internal migration has
a Democratic or Republican effect but that the impact of internal migration depends upon the political tendencies of the states from which the
migrants come: states that draw internal migrants from largely liberal
(conservative), Democratic (Republican) areas are likely to experience
political change in the Democratic (Republican) direction. Chapter 4
expands on this, analyzing the sources of political change in the context of a dynamic model that concentrates on how fluctuations in state
population characteristics are associated with changes in party support.
I focus on some of the commonly cited sources of political change, such
as changes in the racial and ethnic composition of the state electorates, as
well as changes in socioeconomic and occupational status, indicators of
cultural values, and state party identification and ideology. In chapter 5
I shift attention to the changing relationships between population characteristics and election outcomes and how much those changes matter to
state outcomes. In effect I examine how the changing national political
context (party differentiation) has activated demographic and political
characteristics and leads to different outcomes than would have occurred
if the national parties were less differentiated. I also make comparisons
between the effects of compositional and contextual changes on state
political tendencies.

How Does Political
Change Occur?

Chapter 1 outlined a number of important changes in the political complexion of the fifty states: some states moved clearly and substantially in the direction of the Republican Party, others in the Democratic Party direction, and still others changed by smaller degrees or barely registered any change. The challenge now is to develop a framework that helps explain these wide variations in state experiences. How can we explain Vermont's transformation from a state that leaned Republican in the 1970s to a solidly Democratic state in the 2000s, while at the same time explaining Wyoming's movement from solidly Republican to even more Republican, as well as Pennsylvania's and Ohio's continued resistance to change, all in a single theoretical framework? The central argument of this book—that changes in the composition of state populations, along with changes in group-based alignments with political parties, are responsible for changes in state-level patterns of party support in presidential elections—is spelled out in much greater detail in this chapter.

WHAT DO WE KNOW ABOUT PRESIDENTIAL OUTCOMES IN THE STATES?

Although there is scholarship on presidential election outcomes in the states, that body of work has not typically focused on tracking changes in party support across election cycles and does not provide a lot of guidance in this area. Indeed there are virtually no studies that document and try to explain changes in state-level presidential outcomes over time. Some studies have focused very narrowly on specific, transitory stimuli such as voter turnout (Hansford and Gomez 2010), state economic conditions (Brunk and Gough 1983), or candidate home state advantage (Disarro et al. 2007), while others have developed broader models (Holbrook 1991; Rabinowitz et al. 1984), incorporating both long- and short-term influences. A handful of studies have examined the effects of presidential campaigns on state outcomes (Herr 2008; Holbrook and McClurg 2005; Shaw 2008), and a number of others have been less concerned with substantive explanations and more with forecasting state outcomes (Campbell 1992; DeSart and Holbrook 2003; Soumbatiants et al. 2006). As a group these studies tell us that state-level presidential election outcomes in any given year are somewhat easily accounted for by a mix of relatively fixed, long-term influences, such as party and ideology (Holbrook 1991; Rabinowitz et al. 1984; Rosenstone 1983), and more fluid, short-term influences (Holbrook and McClurg 2005; Shaw 2008) that help account for deviations around the long-term tendencies in party support. Importantly these studies tell us that from one election cycle to the next national political tides do not tend to alter the *relative* outcomes across states but instead generate uniform shifts along the lines of "a rising tide lifts all boats" (Campbell 1992; Holbrook 1991). So, for instance, when national conditions augur for a significant Democratic national popular vote margin, traditionally Republican states will still produce outcomes that are *relatively* more Republican than traditionally Democratic states but may shift somewhat in the Democratic direction, as will most other states. In strong Republican years the opposite should happen: traditionally Democratic states are still *relatively* more supportive of the Democratic candidate than other states, but not as supportive as they would be in a neutral or strong Democratic year.

But the sort of change in state outcomes associated with short-term national political tides is not the sort of change that is of interest here. What is much more interesting is long-term changes of the type described in chapter 1, changes that move some states in the Republican direction, others toward the Democrats, and leave some states relatively unscathed. As I noted, however, explaining these types of changes in party fortunes over time has not been a major focus of previous work on state-level outcomes. One exception to this is Holbrook and McClurg's (2005) study of campaign effects, which found that changes in presidential vote share from one election to the next were in part a function of changes in the partisan composition of the electorate; specifically change in Democratic vote share was strongly related to changes in the self-identified Democratic share of the electorate, which itself was responsive to changes in campaign activity. Though this study addressed only short-term, interelection fluctuations, it does offer hints at what might help explain longer-term changes.

REALIGNMENT STUDIES

One body of work that has focused on temporal change, though not always at the state level, is studies of electoral realignment (Burnham 1970; Key 1955; Mayhew 2001, 2002), most of which are primarily concerned with documenting abrupt, election-specific, sometimes seismic shifts in party support across states and in the nation as a whole. The aim of this book is not to document or test ideas about sustained realignments, at least not as usually defined. For instance, realignment studies typically examine "critical" realignments in which a single election cycle produces abrupt and substantial change in party support and in which the previously dominant majority party is replaced by another party, with this new relative balance of power being sustained over time (Burnham 1970; Key 1955; Mayhew 2002). Rather than focusing only on states in which majority status has flipped from one party to another, I place equal emphasis on several different types of outcomes: states in which the dominant party has grown more dominant, states that have witnessed increased competition between the two parties, states that have moved from competitive status to favoring one party over the other, and states that have moved very little. In fact the data presented in chapter 1 show only one clear-cut example of a state (West Virginia) that flipped from decidedly favoring one party to favoring the other.[1] I find that most states have experienced significant change, but those changes flow in myriad directions and with varying degrees of magnitude. It is exactly this variation in political outcomes that makes this an interesting and important question.

While there are empirical and theoretical problems with the concept of critical realignments (Mayhew 2002) and many reasons why the standard conception of a realignment does not fit here, the pattern of change uncovered in chapter 1 and the arguments developed in this chapter fit quite nicely with Key's (1959) notion of a *secular realignment*. Key's (1955) thinking on realignments evolved from developing the concept of critical elections, which produce substantial and sustained shifts in power, to the idea that longer term, somewhat more subtle processes might explain electoral change, that "the rise and fall of parties may to some degree be the consequence of trends that perhaps persist over decades and elections may mark only steps in a more or less continuous creation of new loyalties and decay of old" (Key 1959, 198). A primary thrust of Key's argument identifies changes in group connections to parties as the source of secular realignments, characterizing the essence of this phenomenon as "the fact that a substantial category of persons, defined by a common characteristic, demographic or otherwise, moves over a long period of time toward a partisan homogeneity" (206). In the same vein Key also recognized that some processes could alter the political landscape by diminishing partisan homogeneity within groups (thus changing group alignments) and that changes in the relative size of groups in a geographic area can lead to changes in party strength. Petrocik's (1981, 15) social group model uses a similar characterization of a realignment: "A realignment occurs when the measureable party bias of identifiable segments of the population changes in such a way that the social group profile of the parties—the party coalitions—is altered." The model I develop could easily be thought of as describing something like Key's "secular realignment" or Petrocik's social group model, with an emphasis on both changing population characteristics and changes in how those characteristics matter to election outcomes.

In the same spirit Pomper (1967, 539) developed the idea of a "converting" election, one in which majority party status at the national level remains more or less unchanged but the geographic basis of party strength changes such that each party experiences areas of increased and decreased strength: "The Democratic percentage of the vote, for example, would increase in erstwhile rock-ribbed Republican areas, but would decline in previously Democratic geographical bastions." Pomper describes a process wherein national parties begin to change in ways that create stress on preexisting cleavages and, over time, this stress grows to a point where the contours of partisan cleavages are transformed in a way that "party support and party programs become more congruent"(563). Pomper identifies the 1964 election as an example of a converting election that was the culmination of a process that began with the 1948 Dixiecrat rebellion within the Democratic Party. The Kennedy and Johnson administrations' civil rights policies, as well as the Goldwater candidacy in 1964, exacerbated tensions that began in 1948 and cemented the geographic transformation of party support. Indeed Democratic strength in the South eroded during the 1960s and bounced back only temporarily (and partially) for southern Democratic candidates Jimmy Carter and Bill Clinton.

The primary difference between Pomper's notion of converting elections and Key's notion of secular realignments is that Pomper, to a much greater extent than Key, emphasizes the importance of identifying single election cycles as turning points. The model I have developed resembles Key's conception of secular realignment and Petrocik's notion of changes in party alignment with group cleavages. At the same time, Pomper's more explicit treatment of the impact of changes in party image on voter cleavages, as well as his emphasis on state-based changes in party support flowing in myriad directions, clearly fits the pattern of party change illustrated in chapter 1.

COMPOSITION, CONTEXT, AND POLITICAL CHANGE

The notion of secular realignment has received some attention in discussions of political change across geographic space, even if not explicitly identified as such (Bishop 2009; Gimpel and Schuknecht 2004; Judis and Teixeira 2004). The model presented here reflects many of these ideas, recognizing that what is important politically about geographic space is the characteristics and preferences of the people who occupy the space. If we assume that in any given election year state-level outcomes are driven by the types of people who live in the states and how their characteristics translate into political preferences (with some allowance for short-term influences to push the marker slightly in one direction or another), then explaining change in outcomes over time must incorporate measures of changes in the underlying population characteristics, as well as how those characteristics influence the vote. This is essentially the argument made by Judis and Teixeira (2004), who note that changes in state outcomes, as well as changes in the performance of parties in more localized areas, can be tied to changes in demographic characteristics. Writing over a decade ago, Judis and Teixeira painted a gloomy picture for Republican prospects, largely based on changing demography. Specifically they pointed to the growth of the minority population, as well as the growth of professionals as an occupational category, as harbingers of bad times for Republicans. But central to Judis and Teixeira's model of change is not just that these groups have grown in size but that the connections between groups and parties have changed, largely in response to movement in the ideological center of the parties. Judis and Teixeira point to the increasing prominence of social conservatism in the Republican Party, along with the emergence of the "progressive center" approach of the Democratic Party in the 1990s as the stimulus for changing the nature of group attachments to the parties. The professional class offers a good illustration of this sort of effect.[2] As a group, professionals used to vote solidly Republican, but by the mid-1990s that advantage had disappeared and in some cases tipped toward the Democrats (Brooks and Manza 1997a; Hout et al. 1999; Judis and Teixeira 2004; Manza and Brooks 1999). In Judis and Teixeira's account this happened because professionals are generally socially moderate and are interested in "postindustrial" issues, such as environmental and consumer protection, and not so interested in the agenda of the Religious Right. But changes in party support among professionals resulted not just from their policy preferences but also because the parties moved on related issues. As Judis and Teixeira put it, "Professionals might not have come to the Democratic Party, however, if the party itself had not moved to them" (48). Similarly, in the case of racial and ethnic minorities, issues related to immigration, civil rights, and social welfare programs have served to cement the connection between these groups and the Democratic Party. These are exactly the sorts of issues that some contemporary Republican leaders worry will put these groups even farther outside the reach of their party at the same time these groups are growing in size and political importance (Burns 2013; Gluek 2014; Murphy and Wisecup 2013).

This perspective highlights two important types of effects that form the primary basis of the framework for analyzing changes in party strength in the states. First, there are *compositional effects* due to changes in the demographic, cultural, and political configuration of the population. These are the types of effect that are most commonly articulated in popular discussions of changes in the states, for example, "Colorado is becoming more Democratic because of the increased size of its Latino population." This example emphasizes compositional effects as additive effects: levels of party support change in response to changes in levels of some population characteristic. The other type of effect can be thought of as *contextual effects*, which occur when there are environmental changes that alter the relationship between variables (Marsh 2002; Prysby and Books 1987), for example, "Colorado is becoming more Democratic because Latinos are increasingly aligned with the Democratic Party in response to the parties' positions on immigration." While compositional effects are additive in nature, contextual effects are conditional: the impact of a given population characteristic on party support is conditioned by (or depends upon) the broader political environment.

The conception of compositional effects used here is fairly standard for studies of political geography (Gimpel and Schuknecht 2004; McKee and Teigen 2009), but the conceptualization of contextual effects is somewhat different from what is usually found. Generally studies of context in political geography focus on how some compositional characteristics *of the local area* shape the influence of independent variables (Burbank 1997; Gimpel and Schuknecht 2004; Huckfeldt et al. 1993; Prysby and Books 1987). For instance, Bishop's (2009) argument in *The Big Sort* is that partisan loyalty is much stronger in politically and culturally homogeneous counties than in heterogeneous counties, and Gimpel and Schuknecht (2004) find that Latinos vote as a more cohesive block in states in which they are geographically concentrated than in states where they are more dispersed. This emphasis on *geographic context* is fairly standard in studies of political geography (Agnew 1996) and is sometimes confusingly referred to as a compositional effect (de Vos 1998). In this analysis, however, it is changes in the national political context—specifically increased differentiation of the national parties on policy and ideological grounds—that condition the influence of population characteristics. This fits nicely with Key's (1959) conception of one of the sources of secular realignments, as well as Pomper's (1967) understanding of the impetus for electoral conversion.

The logic of these two types of effects is straightforward, as presented in Table 2.1. The top half of Table 2.1 illustrates the potential impact of changes in the demographic profile of a state, varying the relative size of racial and ethnic groups over time while holding constant the strength of the relationship.[3] In Time 1, white voters make up 81% of the population and there is a clear relationship between race and vote choice, with whites favoring the Republican candidate and minority voters favoring the Democrat. On balance, given the demographic profile and the relationship between group and vote, the Democratic candidate would have a slight edge in this state, garnering roughly 51% of the vote (farthest right column). As time passes and the demographic profile changes, so do the expected vote totals, even if the pattern of support across groups remains the same. This is presented in Time 2, which shows a growth in the minority population (mostly among blacks) and a decline in the white population from 81.2 to 60.8% of the citizen voting age population. Based just on changes in relative group size, the Democratic share of the vote increases by 6 points, to almost 57%.

However, the contextual argument suggests that it is possible that population characteristics could be relatively stable but overall party support could still change if the existing groups shift their loyalties in a way that benefits one party over the other. In the context of the argument I am making, if minority support for the Democrats increases, perhaps in response to the changing party positions on relevant issues, the overall vote share for the Democratic Party could increase, even if the size of the minority population does not change. Consider the two distributions in the bottom half of Table 2.1, which utilize the same population distributions as in the top half but alter the strength of the relationship, with minority groups increasing their attachment to the Democratic Party. Here we see that in both time periods the expected Democratic share of the vote increases in comparison to the corresponding time periods in the top of the table by about 3 percentage points, without any change in the relative size of the population groups. Further, a comparison of Time 1 at the top of the table to Time 2 at the bottom shows the combined influence of both compositional and contextual changes, with the rate of expected Democratic votes increasing by 9 percentage points, from 51 to 60%. This illustrates the potentially powerful impact of compositional and contextual changes when they both favor the same party.

Of course this table is designed to show how compositional and contextual effects related to a single population characteristic *might* produce political changes. This simple, bivariate illustration begs several considerations, however. First, the world isn't so simple that only one thing at a time changes. Indeed over the forty-year swath of political history considered in this book, there have been a number of important changes in population characteristics: changes in occupational status and level of education, in family structure, in union strength, and in religious affiliation, to name just a few. And there have also been changes in how these and other characteristics are aligned with party support (Bafumi and Shapiro 2009; Olson and Green 2008). To the extent that states experience multiple compositional changes in one partisan direction, and to the extent that these changes are amplified by increased electoral relevance of those characteristics, there should be substantial movement toward the favored party. On the other hand, if states experience some changes that augur for increased Democratic support and other changes that suggest greater Republican support, the net effect of demographic change could be offset, resulting in no real change in overall party support. Also, with specific reference to the Table 2.1, it is possible that changes in patterns of

Table 2.1 AN ILLUSTRATION OF THE IMPACT OF COMPOSITIONAL AND
CONTEXTUAL CHANGE ON STATE-LEVEL PRESIDENTIAL OUTCOMES
(HYPOTHETICAL DATA)

Time 1, Weak Relationship

		White	Black	Latino	Other	Total
	Democrat	45%	80%	60%	60%	**51%**
Vote	Republican	55%	20%	40%	40%	**49%**
	Total	**81.2%**	**17.7%**	**0.5%%**	**0.6%**	100%

Time 2, Weak Relationship

		White	Black	Latino	Other	Total
	Democrat	45%	80%	60%	60%	**57%**
Vote	Republican	55%	20%	35%	35%	**43%**
	Total	**60.8%**	**28.9%**	**6.4%**	**3.9%**	100%

Time 1, Stronger Relationship

		White	Black	Latino	Other	Total
	Democrat	45%	93%	70%	70%	**54%**
Vote	Republican	55%	7%	30%	30%	**46%**
	Total	**81.2%**	**17.7%**	**0.5%**	**0.6%**	100%

Time 2, Stronger Relationship

		White	Black	Latino	Other	Total
	Democrat	45%	93%	70%	70%	**60%**
Vote	Republican	55%	7%	30%	30%	**40%**
	Total	**60.8%**	**28.9%**	**6.4%**	**3.9%**	100%

support across categories of a single variable, such as race and ethnicity, could be offsetting. For instance, if minority voters grow more supportive of Democratic candidates in response to party positions on race-related issues, it is certainly plausible that Democrats would lose support among white voters, perhaps in great enough magnitude to offset the changes in behavior of minority voters in response to the same set of issues. This has certainly been the case among white southerners (Black 2004; Black and

Black 2009; Carmines and Stimson 1989; Hayes and McKee 2008; Miller 1991; Petrocik 1981, 1987) and, to a lesser degree, in the rest of the country. To the extent that this happens, the effects of variables such as race and ethnicity may be muted.

THE ROOTS OF COMPOSITIONAL CHANGE

How do compositional changes occur? States (or any geographic units) don't change simply with the passage of time; instead there are different processes at work. Over time compositional changes in standard demographic characteristics are most likely to occur in two ways: through *migration* and *generational replacement*. Of course both processes are at work in all fifty states. Migration-based effects on political outcomes occur when state residents who were born elsewhere and migrated to the state are different in politically relevant ways from residents who were born in the state. Migrants may be internal (born in another state) or external (born in another country). Some academic research has addressed the political consequences of migration, coming to somewhat different conclusions. Gimpel and Schucknecht (2001, 2004) make a strong argument in their county-level analysis of gubernatorial and presidential elections that, based on the characteristics of internal migrants, the expected effect of internal migration should be a net benefit to the Republican Party. Though they do not find this in every instance and conclude that the impact of migration is likely to depend on where migrants came from and why they moved, their evidence, on balance, generally supports the idea of in-migration as a benefit to Republicans (Gimpel and Schuknecht 2001). Others, however, suggest that the impact of migration may not be quite so clear. Jurjevich and Plane (2012) examine the "political effectiveness" of migration, focusing on the tendency of net-migration patterns to either strengthen or dilute existing partisan strengths. They find that there is no simple, consistent answer to who benefits from migration, concluding, "Our results suggest migration streams are not just *sometimes* more plural and heterogeneous than the literature suggests, but *often* more plural and *considerably* more diverse" (442). Hood and McKee (2010) use a combination of survey data and data from party registration records to study the impact of migration patterns on the 2008 presidential outcome in North Carolina. They find that nonnatives were somewhat more liberal, had higher levels of education, were less religious, and were more likely to register as Independents than native North Carolinians. In aggregate the effect of the growing nonnative population helped seal Obama's 2008 victory in North Carolina (Hood and McKee 2010). In addition, Robinson and Noriega (2010) have tied the migration of highly educated professionals to improved Democratic prospects at the county level in several Mountain West states. This finding fits the larger point from Jurjevich and Plane (2012), that there is no single direction of partisan benefit from migration between states. Instead the impact of migration is likely to vary from state to state and to depend upon groups represented in the migration streams and where they are migrating from.

Migration does, however, play a key role in changing the demographic makeup of a state. How it affects elections is likely a function of the scale of migration and from where those migrants come. In cases in which the preponderance of migration is from Democratic or liberal states to Republican or conservative states, the net effect of migration should be to move the destination states in a Democratic direction. And of course if the flow were in the other direction, the net effect should be to move the destination states toward the Republican Party. These effects should be greater in cases in which migrants constitute a significant share of the total state population. Robinson and Noriega (2010) find exactly this in their study of the influence of voter migration on changes in county-level Democratic support in Mountain West states. Counties that experienced the greatest influx of internal migrants from other counties with greater Democratic strength tended to grow more Democratic over time. We should also recognize that the partisan and ideological makeup of the destination state could have an impact on the migrants. While most studies have focused on the potential for migration to alter the complexion of destination states, it is also possible that the context of the destination states can have an impact on those who migrate. Brown's (1988) early work in this area focused on the impact of destination-county partisan environments on the partisanship of recent migrants, finding that migrants tend to calibrate their partisanship somewhat to suit the prevailing local environment. More recent work (MacDonald and Franko 2008) has extended this framework to examine the impact of the statewide partisan environment on migrants, again finding a tendency among migrants to move slightly in the direction of the dominant party orientation of their destination state. To the extent that these sorts of effects exist, they will serve to dampen the effects of migration from states of differing partisan composition.

Migration is only one mechanism for changing the population characteristics of the states. As mentioned earlier, generational replacement is another possible source of influence, perhaps working in concert with migration patterns. Over time, as new groups make up a larger share of the population, subsequent generations of those groups may take up even larger shares, especially if there are group-based differences in birth rates. Generational replacement could be especially important to understanding change in nondemographic population characteristics that are more clearly political in nature, such as party affiliation and political ideology. If new generations of voters come to political age unfettered by decades of identification with a locally dominant political party, especially during times of political change, their politics stand a good chance of being different from that of preceding generations (Miller and Shanks 1996). The transformation of party politics in the American South in response to the changing party positions on racial and social welfare issues provides one example of the potential impact of generational replacement in the transformation of geographic areas (Carmines and Stimson 1989; Hayes and McKee 2008; Miller 1991). As the two major parties separated on issues related to race and civil rights, new generations of otherwise conservative voters in the South were freer to abandon previous generations' longtime— though increasingly strained—commitment to the Democratic Party in favor of the Republican Party, whose general orientation and specific positions on issues of race were a better fit for them. A similar, though not as substantial effect of generational replacement has been found in the northeastern states, where changes in the political positions of the parties on race and social welfare issues led to important generational replacement effects and transformed the region from a Republican stronghold to a bastion of Democratic strength (Bullock et al. 2006; Knuckey 2009).

This set of findings raises an important point about compositional change in the states. While it is typical for compositional analyses to focus primarily on standard demographic categories such as race, sex, education, and occupational status, states also differ in terms of underlying political preferences, and these preferences can change over time. States are not individuals and as such don't have preferences in the same sense that individuals do. But to the extent that a state's population leans decidedly toward the Democratic or Republican Party or has policy preferences that are decidedly liberal or conservative in aggregate, those differences will be reflected in election outcomes at the state level. This is hardly earth-shattering or a profoundly new proposition regarding state politics, but it is important to understand that compositional changes in state populations can encompass much more than just demographic categories and should also include the underlying partisan and ideological makeup of the population. We know that states differ on partisan and ideological dimensions and that these differences play an important role in shaping election outcomes in the states (Holbrook 1991; Holbrook and McClurg 2005; Rabinowitz et al. 1984; Rosenstone 1983). By almost any measure of state partisanship or state political ideology, states in which the Democratic presidential candidates have won by the widest margins in recent years (Hawaii, New York, Massachusetts, Rhode Island, Vermont) tend to be states that have the highest levels of Democratic Party affiliation or liberal ideological identification, just as states in which the Republican candidates have won by the widest margins (Idaho, Nebraska, Oklahoma, Utah, Wyoming) are among the most Republican and conservative states (Enns and Koch 2013; Pacheco 2011). Again this is hardly a new discovery, but it is very important to take into account when considering how changes in these underlying characteristics may have contributed to changes in presidential outcomes in the states. We know that even short-term changes (between election cycles) in the partisan composition of the electorate can have important effects on presidential outcomes in the states (Holbrook and McClurg 2005), so it seems especially important to take into account changes of this nature over the long haul. It is also important to acknowledge that changes in underlying state political positions are partly in response to changes in important demographic characteristics. This connection will be incorporated into the analysis of the impact of compositional change on election outcomes.

To be clear, the expectations for the analysis of compositional change are that changes over time in key statewide population characteristics lead to changes over time in statewide party support in presidential elections. The discussion and justification of precisely which population characteristics are important is presented in the next couple of chapters, but these characteristics generally reflect socioeconomic and occupational status, race and ethnicity, and cultural indicators and characteristics that respond to cultural issues and political predispositions. While it is important to understand the processes that contribute to population change, the primary emphasis is on the effects of population change on changes in votes. However, changes in migratory patterns also are given significant attention both as a source of change in other population characteristics and as a population characteristic in and of itself.

SOURCES OF CONTEXTUAL EFFECTS

Recall that the use of *context* here is different from the standard use of the term in studies of political geography. Whereas studies of contextual effects in political geography typically focus on the impact of geographic space on behavioral relationships, the focus here is on something perhaps better called temporal, or global, contextual effects. One of the clearest illustrations of this sort of process is found in Carmines and Stimson's (1989) *Issue Evolution*. In their account of how racial policy transformed the mass membership of the Democratic and Republican parties, Carmines and Stimson spell out a simple but elegant process. First, parties separate on an issue in a way that differs from their previous alignment; then this separation provides issue "clarity" for the mass public and facilitates the public's ability to differentiate between the parties. This clarity then leads to shifting bases of party support as groups use the information to align their interests and preferences with party positions. In the specific case of racial politics, once the parties began to separate in the late 1950s, the mass public became increasingly aware of newly liberal positions on race issues for the Democratic Party and newly conservative positions for the Republican Party, leading some voters, especially southern whites, to grow increasingly disenchanted with the Democratic Party. At the same time, African American voters, who were already in the Democratic camp, became even more solidly Democratic in their orientation. The relationship between race and party identification and vote choice changed in response to changes in party positions. Carmines and Stimson are not alone in their view of how racial politics transformed southern support for the Democratic Party and contributed to a secular realignment along the lines of race in American politics (Black 2004; Black and Black 2009; Miller 1991). Though their primary focus was on race-related policies, Carmines and Stimson's model more broadly illuminates the process by which the national political context can alter underlying relationships between demographic characteristics and party support. This approach has been useful in other issue domains as well. For instance, Adams (1997) found that as party reputations on abortion became more distinct throughout the 1970s and 1980s, the relationship between attitude toward abortion and party support changed as well, again indicating a strong connection between elite positions and mass identification. Carmines et al. (2010) also explored the issue evolution of abortion, finding that one of the key pieces in the process was media coverage of the interactions between political elites from both parties and interest groups aligned on opposite sides of the abortion issue. These studies reaffirm the public's ability to sniff out important changes in party positions and, over time, align accordingly.[4]

Undergirding the model of issue evolution is the idea that mass political behavior responds to elite signals. This idea is not unique to issue evolution and plays an important role in studies of attitude formation (Bullock 2011; Zaller 1991) and political polarization (Abramowitz and Saunders 2008; Fiorina et al. 2004; Levendusky 2009, 2010). For instance, Fiorina et al.'s account of the emergence of new issue or social cleavages in voting behavior emphasizes that changes in voting behavior may be attributed to changes in candidate behavior rather than changes in voters themselves. By this account, important underlying issue positions or identities may exist among voters but play a small part in elections if candidates themselves are not known to differ on the relevant issue or if that issue plays a very small part in the campaign. Again abortion is a good example of an issue on which voters may have held strong opinions but was not clearly connected to party affiliation or vote choice until the parties diverged on this issue in the 1970s (Adams 1997). Likewise Levendusky (2009) shows that elite ideological polarization throughout the 1980s, 1990s, and 2000s facilitated partisan sorting such that "misplaced" conservative Democrats found their way to the Republican Party and "misplaced" liberal Republicans found their way to the Democratic Party, increasing the connection between mass ideology and mass party affiliation. As Levendusky puts it, one of the benefits of elite polarization is that it "helps voters figure out 'what goes with what' and allows them to make sense of the political world" (9). There is abundant evidence to support this proposition. For instance, Hetherington's (2001) analysis of the resurgence in party identification as a voting cue demonstrates that partisan voting is directly linked to the increased polarization of congressional parties. Weinschenk's (2014) analysis of voting behavior in congressional elections uses a group conflict framework and finds that increased ideological conflict between party elites has heightened the connection between voter ideology and candidate choice in U.S. House elections. And although they don't pin all changes on elite polarization, Bafumi and Shapiro's (2009) analysis of the "new partisan voter" documents multiple changes in group–based party alignments at the individual level that track well with increases in elite polarization.

Rabinowitz et al. (1984) have documented a similar sort of process in state-level presidential election outcomes. Their primary objective was to uncover and differentiate between the partisan and ideological structure of state-level presidential election outcomes. What they found was clear evidence of both partisan and ideological dimensions but that the ideological dimension supplanted partisanship over time and came to dominate state-level outcomes beginning in the 1960s. Rabinowitz et al. argue that the importance of the ideology dimension depended on the placement of candidates on issue dimensions. When candidates occupied relatively proximate space on the ideological dimension, ideology took on less importance, and as candidates diverged in ideological space, ideology grew in importance. By their account, this is exactly what happened during the 1960s. As southern Democrats faced increasingly liberal Democratic presidential candidates and a Democratic Party that was increasingly liberal on racial issues, state partisan leanings became less important to state outcomes and state ideology became increasingly important. This squares quite nicely with Carmines and Stimson's (1989) work on issue evolution and is in the same spirit as other work on the importance of elite actions for mass political behavior (Abramowitz 2010; Adams 1997; Fiorina et al. 2004; Levendusky 2009, 2010; Zaller 1991).[5]

This is not a book about issue evolution or political polarization per se but rather, in part, about how a similar sort of process has affected group connections to parties and candidates. Think of it as something like an elite-driven *demographic sort*, whereby groups are sorting into clearer alignment with the parties. The basic idea is similar to that of the partisan sort (Levendusky 2009): just as elite ideological polarization facilitated increased interparty differentiation along ideological lines at the mass level, it should also facilitate connections among group interests, group preferences, and parties. Here it is important to distinguish between interests and preferences. Some groups have well-delineated common interests that can be easily connected to the parties, while other groups are defined by some shared characteristic but may be more or less attracted to parties on the basis of a common liberal or conservative worldview (Petrocik 1981). Consider, for example, Judis and Teixeira's (2004) account of the different ways racial minorities and the professional class have become more closely connected to the Democratic Party: changes in party positions on civil rights, affirmative action, and immigration policy have heightened the relationship between race and ethnicity and party support, leading to increased levels of Democratic support among racial and ethnic minorities and decreased levels of support among white voters. In this case it seems clear that a substantial basis for the transformation of these groups lies in the connection between group interests and party positions. Such is also the case in the relationship between union membership and party support and that between income and party support.

At the same time, some movement that appears to be related to group interests might also reflect how changes in party positions have activated other underlying preferences or sensibilities that coincide with group distinctions. For instance, to the extent that racial animus exists among some white voters, it is likely to be activated by growing party differentiation on policies related to race and ethnicity (Kinder and Sanders 1996; Tesler and Sears 2010) and contribute to disenchantment with the Democratic Party, at least among some white voters. Also consider so-called cultural issues, such as abortion and gay rights, or more generally the increased importance of the Christian conservative movement, embraced by the Republican establishment beginning in the late 1970s (Bishop 2009; Milkis et al. 2013; Pieper 2011). Increased differentiation between the parties on these issues may be responsible for altering group-based connections to the parties even though these issues may not be directly related to group interests but tap into important group differences in preferences. For instance, part of the explanation for the decline of the Democratic Party among working-class whites is typically attributed to partisan differences on cultural issues (Abramowitz and Teixeira 2009; Bishop 2009), leading culturally conservative whites to align more consistently with the culturally conservative Republican Party.

This sort of activation of preferences and sensibilities seems especially clear in the case of the professional class. Although people whose occupation could be classified as professional are likely to have moderate to conservative views on economic issues, and certainly their level of income would seem to put them at odds with Democratic economic policies, they tend to have moderate to liberal views on social and cultural issues (Manza and Brooks 1999).[6] In Judis and Teixeira's (2004) account, as the parties diverged on these issues, they assumed a more prominent role in decision making, and the professional class moved toward the Democratic Party in response. Again the important distinction is that this type of group change is related not to group interest but to the political tastes of the group.

As the distance between the parties grows greater, not only should well-defined groups in society find it easier to make interest-based connections to the parties, but more generally it also should become easier for people to connect their policy preferences to the parties. Just as the literature on the partisan sort has found that ideology and party identification grew more closely connected as elite party cues on ideology became clearer and more consistent (Abramowitz 2010; Levendusky 2009, 2010), demographic groups with well-defined interests or homogeneous political worldviews also should line up more consistently behind increasingly differentiated political parties.

SUMMARY

As we saw in chapter 1, the political landscape of presidential elections has undergone an important and substantial transformation in the past forty years. Though movement has been in both directions—some states moving decidedly in the Republican direction, others in the Democratic direction—these changes have been a net benefit for the Democratic Party. It is unlikely that any single variable can explain these changes, especially given the heterogeneous pattern of change. Instead I propose two different plausible explanations for the observed changes in the geographic contours of party support in presidential elections: compositional effects, which focus on changes in state characteristics, and contextual effects, which focus on change in how those characteristics matter to election outcomes. Importantly these two explanations are not mutually exclusive and both can shape the changing electoral profiles of the fifty states.

It might be beneficial to think about compositional and contextual effects by recasting the patterns shown in Table 2.1 within the framework of a linear model of presidential vote shares at the state level:

$$Vote_i = \beta_0 + \beta_1 X_i \tag{2.1}$$

where $Vote_i$ is the Democratic share of the two-party presidential vote in state i, β_0 is a constant, X_i is some state characteristic in state i, and β_1 is a slope that tells how much the Democratic share of the vote in a given state will increase or decrease for every unit change in X. So how do we produce change in the Democratic share of the vote? Changes in β_0 will produce changes in Democratic vote share, but these changes will be uniform across states and hence cannot help explain why states have moved in different directions or experience differences in the magnitude of change. Changes in β_0 likely reflect something like national political tides, which can change from one election cycle to the next but probably don't disturb the *relative* levels of support across states. Instead the types of change I want to explain are likely to be produced by changes in β_1 or changes in X_i. The compositional model emphasizes changing values of X_i as the source of change in votes, analogous to the effects illustrated in the top half of Table 2.1. The contextual model emphasizes changes in β_1 as the source of political change, analogous to the effects shown by comparing the top and bottom parts of Table 2.1. If changes in β_1 and X_i point in the same partisan direction, change in Democratic vote share should be relatively pronounced; if changes in both are offsetting or relatively small in scale, then change in Democratic vote share should be relatively limited.

There are multiple processes that can produce change in state characteristics over time, including migration patterns and generational replacement. My analysis focuses on migration patterns from both internal (other states) and external (foreign countries) sources. Changes in slopes are expected to follow changes in the behavior of national party elites; as parties diverge ideologically, it is expected that state demographic and political characteristics will become more strongly related to state-level outcomes. Of course the world is more complicated than just one slope and one independent variable. In next two chapters I investigate how changes in multiple state characteristics (X_is) are connected to changes in state-level presidential election outcomes. Following this I examine the extent to which the relationships between state characteristics and election outcomes (β_1s) have changed and also estimate the impact of those changes on Democratic share of the state-level presidential votes.

Population Migration and Political Change

In this chapter I examine how changes in the composition of state populations contribute to changes over time in patterns of political support for presidential candidates across the states. The strategy I use is to take a closer look at migratory patterns to get a handle on the extent to which migration from state to state, as well as immigration from outside the United States, alters the political landscape of the states. This involves identifying characteristics and categories of migrants that are likely to have the greatest impact on political outcomes and then assessing the direct effects of migration on political change. This focus on migration provides insights into an important process that contributes to changes in other population characteristics, which are examined in greater detail in chapter 4.

As discussed in chapter 2, population migration is an important potential source of political change in the states. While population characteristics in a given state can change over time without significant in-migration, perhaps through generational replacement and differential birth rates across groups, they also can change as new people move to the state either from other states or from foreign countries. The impact of migration is likely to depend on the overall scope of migration and the extent to which new state residents are different from state natives in politically relevant ways (Gimpel and Schuknecht 2004; Jurjevich and Plane 2012; Robinson and Noriega 2010). In states in which there is relatively little in-migration the differences between migrant and native populations would have to be quite stark in order to produce substantively important political change. On the other hand, in states with substantial levels of in-migration, even somewhat modest differences between migrant and native populations could move the state in one or the other political direction. And of course the most substantial impact would occur in states with substantial levels of in-migration and in which the migrant and native populations were substantially different in politically relevant ways.

THE SCOPE OF MIGRATION

The maps presented in Figure 3.1 and the data in Table 3.1 shed light on part of this equation, illustrating the scope and sources of population migration across the states. These data are based on estimates from the 2012 American Community Survey of the percentage of each state's citizen voting-age population (CVAP) born outside the state.[1] The CVAP is used as the base here and for most of the other population statistics in this chapter. This is done for a couple of reasons. First, for some variables related to race, ethnicity, and migration, a significant share of the population of interest is not eligible to participate in elections due to citizenship status. Using CVAP as the basis for measuring relative group size focuses on that part of the population that is likely to have the greatest impact on political outcomes: those who are eligible to vote.[2] More detailed information on the measurement of state characteristics is provided in the appendix.

The top map in Figure 3.1 (see also the first column of data in Table 3.1) makes clear that the potential for migration to affect political change varies considerably across the states, based on the scope of in-migration. States with dark shading have the highest levels of in-migration, and states with light shading have the lowest levels of in-migration. As a point of reference, nationwide in 2012, 43% of the CVAP were living somewhere other than the state or nation where they were born, a level

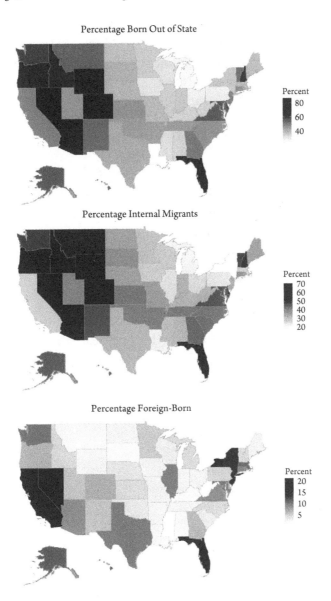

Figure 3.1 Size and Sources of the Migrant Population in the States, 2012

NOTE: Each map uses a different scale due to differences in the range of each measure of migration. All maps were created using Choroplethr.

that would register on the lighter end of the scale. There are a couple of different patterns to note here. First, generally migration is tied to population growth: the correlation between state population growth from 1970 to 2010 and the percentage of state population born out of

Table 3.1 BREAKDOWN OF THE CITIZEN VOTING-AGE POPULATION BY MIGRATION STATUS BY STATE, 2012

State	Percentage Born Outside of State	Percentage Born in Other States	Percentage Foreign-Born
Alabama	32.0	29.8	2.2
Alaska	67.5	61.5	6.0
Arizona	71.4	62.7	8.7
Arkansas	41.7	39.2	2.5
California	47.3	25.8	21.5
Colorado	65.8	59.1	6.7
Connecticut	46.4	37.0	9.4
Delaware	60.9	54.7	6.2
Florida	71.9	56.9	15.0
Georgia	48.7	42.6	6.1
Hawaii	47.3	31.5	15.8
Idaho	60.1	56.0	4.1
Illinois	33.0	23.4	9.6
Indiana	33.8	31.3	2.5
Iowa	28.8	26.2	2.6
Kansas	44.0	39.9	4.1
Kentucky	31.8	30.0	1.8
Louisiana	22.3	20.0	2.3
Maine	37.1	34.3	2.8
Maryland	56.0	45.9	10.1
Massachusetts	37.5	26.4	11.1
Michigan	24.3	19.9	4.4
Minnesota	33.6	28.5	5.1
Mississippi	30.4	29.1	1.3
Missouri	36.7	34.1	2.6
Montana	52.3	50.3	2.0
Nebraska	36.9	33.3	3.6
Nevada	86.1	72.0	14.1
New Hampshire	63.8	59.6	4.2
New Jersey	48.9	32.3	16.6

Table 3.1 CONTINUED

State	Percentage Born Outside of State	Percentage Born in Other States	Percentage Foreign-Born
New Mexico	51.4	45.9	5.5
New York	35.0	16.9	18.1
North Carolina	44.7	40.6	4.1
North Dakota	35.7	33.3	2.4
Ohio	27.1	24.3	2.8
Oklahoma	42.3	39.1	3.2
Oregon	60.2	54.2	6.0
Pennsylvania	26.7	22.3	4.4
Rhode Island	43.4	34.0	9.4
South Carolina	44.8	41.7	3.1
South Dakota	38.3	36.4	1.9
Tennessee	42.7	40.0	2.7
Texas	39.5	29.8	9.7
Utah	42.7	37.4	5.3
Vermont	52.2	48.3	3.9
Virginia	54.4	45.7	8.7
Washington	57.6	47.5	10.1
West Virginia	31.5	30.2	1.3
Wisconsin	29.8	26.9	2.9
Wyoming	66.5	64.2	2.3
Fifty-state Average	45.3	39.0	6.3

NOTE: All data are taken from the 2012 American Community Survey.

state in 2012 is .75. This is not universally the case—for instance, Utah and Texas have relatively modest in-migration rates, given their population growth rates—but generally states that grew the most tend to have larger nonnative populations. Second, there is a regional pattern to the size of the nonnative population, no doubt also reflecting differences in population growth: Mountain West and southwestern states, along with Florida and several southeastern states, have higher in-migration, and the industrial Midwest and Northeast and parts of the Deep South tend to have smaller state-native populations. Third, in a handful of states the size of the native population is swamped by that of the population born out of state: states with the largest nonnative populations are Nevada (86%), Florida (72%), Arizona (71%), Alaska (68%), Wyoming (67%), and Colorado (66%). At the other extreme a number of states have relatively few residents who were born elsewhere: Louisiana (22%), Michigan (24%), Pennsylvania (27%), Ohio (27%), Wisconsin (30%), and Mississippi (30%). These patterns, in part, reflect the industrial decline of Rust Belt states and increased economic opportunities in the southeastern and western states.

It also is important to make distinctions regarding the sources of these migration patterns. In very broad terms the nonnative population in any given state is composed of people who were born in other states or U.S. territories (internal migrants) and people who were born outside of the United States (foreign-born). In 2012, 34% of the CVAP were internal migrants, and 9% were born in a foreign country. This distinction is important because internal migrants and foreign-born residents are likely to differ on characteristics that could have important political consequences. The distinction is also important because there are substantial differences in the type of state that tends to attract more internal versus foreign-born migrants. The second map in Figure 3.1 (second column of data in Table 3.1) shows the distribution of internal migrants as a percentage of state CVAP. It looks a lot like the top map, with a couple of prominent exceptions: New Hampshire emerges as one of the states in which internal migrants constitute a relatively high percentage of the state's population (60%), and New York as the state with the smallest concentration of internal migrants, at 17%. Otherwise the pattern is familiar, with the Mountain states, southwestern states, Florida, and southeastern states with high concentrations of internal migrants.

The picture is appreciably different, however, when considering foreign-born population as a percentage of state population (bottom map in Figure 3.1, third column of Table 3.1). In this case a handful of states stand out as having the highest percentage of their population born outside the United States: California (22%), New York (18%), New Jersey (16%), Hawaii (16%), Florida (15%), and Nevada (14%). Together these states account for the destination of 55% of the foreign-born CVAP. By comparison, these same states account for only 26% of the internal migrant population. States in which the foreign-born constitute a relatively small share of the state population are found primarily in the Midwest (with the exception of Illinois), the Plains states, and the Border South and Mississippi Delta states. A handful of states (Kentucky, Mississippi, Montana, South Dakota, and West Virginia) had foreign-born CVAP of 2% or less.

DEMOGRAPHIC CHANGE AND MIGRATION

Although the impact of migration on political change in the states is likely a function of the size of the overall migrant population in any given state, it is also likely to be a function of the extent to which migrants are different from natives in politically relevant ways. These differences vary somewhat from state to state, but we can get a sense of their potential importance by examining them over time for the nation as a whole. Table 3.2 provides a glimpse into potentially relevant demographic and attitudinal characteristics of three different groups: foreign-born migrants, internal migrants, and people who live in the state where they were born (natives). Included here are measures of standard demographic characteristics: educational attainment, occupational status, race and ethnicity, marital status, poverty rate, and age. Also included are two measures of political attitudes: net party identification (percent Democratic identifiers minus percent Republican identifiers) and net ideology (percent liberal identifiers minus percent conservative identifiers). These data are examined in two different time periods—1970–80 and 2004–12—that bookend the changes in party support examined in chapter 1. With this table we are able to examine demographic and attitudinal differences

Table 3.2 SELECTED CHARACTERISTICS OF MIGRANT AND NONMIGRANT POPULATIONS, 1970–80 AND 2004–12

Characteristics	1970–80			2004–12		
	Foreign-Born	Internal Migrants	State Natives	Foreign-Born	Internal Migrants	State Natives
% BA	4	7	5	20	21	15
% Advanced Degree	4	5	3	13	13	7
% Management	10	9	8	13	16	11
% Professional	10	11	9	19	21	15
% White	86	86	88	28	78	73
% Black	2	11	9	9	11	14
% Latino	9	2	2	31	8	9
% Other Races	4	1	1	32	8	9
% Single	9	15	19	18	24	34
% Poverty	14	13	12	12	12	14
Average Age	58	44	43	50	50	45
% Dem–% Rep	+26	+10	+22	+27	0	–10
% Lib–% Con	–2	–8	–6	–1	–13	–9
% of Total	5	42	53	8	35	57

NOTE: Demographic data are based on estimates from the decennial census for 1970 to 1980 and the American Community Surveys for 2004 to 2012. Data on party affiliation and ideology are taken from the General Social Survey (GSS), using data from 1977–80 and 2004–12. The census data represent estimates for the CVAP, while the GSS data represent estimates for the voting-age population. For party identification and ideology, both of which are drawn from GSS data, the internal migrant data represent the status of people whose current state of residence is different from where they lived when they were sixteen years old. More details on data gathering are provided in the appendix.

across migration-based groups and changes in group-based differentiation over time.

Looking first at the early period, there were relatively few substantial demographic differences by migration status: the group differences in educational attainment and occupational status were relatively slight; all three groups were overwhelmingly white, with Latinos constituting a somewhat greater share of the foreign-born population than internal migrants or state natives; and foreign-born were somewhat less likely to be single and were on average about fifteen years older than native-born CVAP. In terms of party identification and political ideology, internal migrants were somewhat less Democratic and more conservative than were foreign-born and state natives, while all three groups tilted Democratic and also slightly conservative to varying degrees.[3] All in all, the differences are relatively small, and those differences that do exist sometimes pull in different directions. For instance, foreign-born residents might be expected to be somewhat less likely to support Democratic candidates based on their marital status and age, but they have a higher level of Democratic identification and are (slightly) less conservative than native-born residents, which should point them toward the Democratic camp.

The group differences are much more dramatic in the later time period: both foreign-born residents and internal migrants have higher levels of educational and occupational status than state natives; whites constitute a relatively small minority among the foreign-born population, trailing behind Latinos and "other" racial and ethnic groups; and differences in political attitudes grew substantially in magnitude, perhaps as a result of these demographic changes. At a time when internal migrants and state natives grew more Republican and more conservative, foreign-born residents maintained their allegiance to the Democratic Party and also barely changed on the ideological front. The change in the racial and ethnic composition of foreign-born residents is particularly notable, reflecting a substantial difference between the two time periods in the geographic basis of immigration from other countries. Data from the 1970 and 1980 census studies show that, at that time, fully 61% of the foreign-born CVAP came from Europe, 13% from Latin America, 9% from Asia, 1% from Africa, and 16% from other areas (e.g., Canada, Australia). For the period from 2004 to 2012 data from the American Community Surveys show that 37% of the foreign-born CVAP came from Latin America, 35% from Asia, 21% from Europe, 4% from Africa, and the rest from elsewhere. The internal migrant population from 2004 to 2012 provides a bit of a mixed picture: it looks very much like the foreign-born population in terms of education, occupation, average age, and marital status but is more similar to state natives on race, ethnicity, and political attitudes, though leaning somewhat more Democratic and at the same time somewhat more conservative.

On balance, these differences support the expectation that states with a substantial foreign-born population should see increases in Democratic support from the 1970s to the 2010s. Also, given the increasing differences between foreign-born and other citizens over time, we should see important changes in the relationship between the percentage of foreign-born and Democratic vote shares over time. At the same time, it is not clear that the level of internal migration in a state necessarily should benefit one party or the other, at least based on characteristics of the migrating population compared to those who have not moved across state lines. There are some differences between internal migrants and native state residents, but perhaps not large enough to produce significant change without taking a more nuanced look at how internal migrants differ from state to state.

MIGRATION AND ELECTION OUTCOMES

We can begin to get a sense of the impact of migration on political change by looking at the simple bivariate relationships between migration differences among the states and changes in Democratic performance in state-level presidential outcomes. Before decomposing state population by source of migration, it is useful to examine the impact of migration overall on state outcomes. The top left panel of Figure 3.2 examines change in Democratic vote as a function of the percentage of the state population born out of state. The change in Democratic vote summarizes the state-by-state regression slopes presented in Figures 1.3 and 1.4. Instead of using the slopes themselves (which can be intuitively cumbersome) as the dependent variable, this figure looks at the change in the average estimated centered Democratic vote from 1972–80 to 2004–12, which is derived from the slopes.[4] These averages are also the same as the difference between the starting and end points of arrows representing state change in Figure 1.5. The horizontal axis in the top left panel of Figure 3.2 represents the total nonnative population (CVAP) of the states in 2008, the midpoint of the contemporary election period measured in the dependent variable. This includes both internal migrants and foreign-born state residents. Here we see that, by looking at overall migration without considering the sources of migration, the impact on change in party support is relatively paltry. There is a slight positive trend to these data (r = .34), suggesting that Democrats have made modest gains in states with the highest percentage of residents who are internal or external migrants. But this is not a strong relationship and surely does not explain much of the Democratic gains and losses over time.

This overall view of the impact of migration may be a bit misleading in that it assumes that migration effects are constant across migrant groups, an assumption that is likely in error considering the demographic and political profiles of the migrant groups provided in Table 3.2. Given its distinct racial, ethnic, and political makeup, the foreign-born population would seem to be the most obvious place to start. The top right panel in Figure 3.2 presents the relationship between the percentage of the state citizen voting-age population who are foreign-born in 2008 and change in Democratic performance in state-level residential outcomes from 1972–80 to 2004–12. Here we see a much more dramatic relationship. Generally speaking, states in which the foreign-born population constitutes a relatively large share of the CVAP also tend to be states in which the Democratic Party has significantly improved its position over time

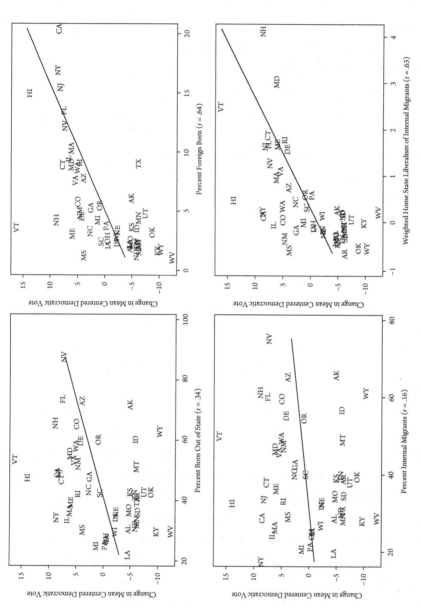

Figure 3.2 The Influence of Population Migration on Changes in Democratic Support, 1972–76 to 2004–12

NOTE: The dependent variable is change in estimated Democratic support from 1972–80 to 2004–12, based on the trend in the Democratic share of the two-party vote, centered around the national two-party division (see Figures 1.3 and 1.4). All independent variables are measured based on migration patterns in 2008. Weighted home-state liberalism is calculated using Equation 3.1.

(r = .64). Although the prediction line is linear, there is a bit of a curvilinear trend in the data: among states with a relatively small foreign-born population (1 to 5%) there is a mix of political outcomes, though most states saw a decline in Democratic strength; beyond that point (greater than 5% foreign-born) there is a much stronger tendency for higher levels of the foreign-born population to be associated with greater Democratic success. One noteworthy exception is Texas, which had above-average levels of foreign-born population and a substantial decline in Democratic support. Otherwise there are no states with high levels of foreign-born population and declining Democratic electoral strength, leading to the completely empty lower right quadrant of the scatter plot. The size of the foreign-born population appears to provide a particularly good explanation for changes in Democratic strength for a number of states with especially high levels of foreign-born population: California, Florida, Massachusetts, Nevada, New Jersey, and New York all fall very close to a prediction line. One other state that stands out as a bit of an anomaly is Vermont, where Democrats made their largest electoral gains, but where there is also very little foreign-born population to speak of. Obviously something else must be driving political change in Vermont. Otherwise the size of the foreign-born population appears to be an important part of the explanation for why Democrats improve their lot in some states more than others.

The key to this relationship is not just that some states have higher levels foreign-born population, but that higher concentrations of foreign-born population are connected to other politically relevant changes in state characteristics. For instance, Table 3.2 shows clear educational, occupational, and racial and ethnic differences between the foreign-born and native populations. States that experience changes in their foreign-born population should experience concomitant changes in these politically relevant characteristics.

The expectations are less clear for the influence of internal migrants on political change, given that they are not much different from the state native populations, at least on racial, ethnic, and political dimensions. This is borne out by the data in the lower left panel of Figure 3.2, which uses the percentage of the CVAP in 2008 who were internal migrants as the independent variable and change in Democratic support as the dependent variable. There is no clear pattern in this figure, certainly not one that rises to the level of being either statistically significant or substantively interesting (r = .16, p = .28). This null finding likely is an illustration of the fallacy of considering only the volume of internal migration without regard for the nature of the migrants. This figure ignores the possibility that the characteristics of internal migrants may differ from state to state in ways that have important political consequences. Consider, for example, Robinson and Noriega's (2010) work on county-level migration in the Mountain West states. In responding to previous work that found overall migration levels were not related to changes in party success at the county level, Robinson and Noriega proffered that it is not enough to simply look at the levels of in-migration; it also is necessary to examine where those migrants came from. Specifically they took into account the partisan leanings of counties from which the migrants came and found that in-migration, weighted by the political leanings of the source counties, was strongly related to political change at the county level.

It is likely that the same sort of process is at work in the states. If a given state has a high level of internal migration, but those migrants come from a diverse set of states with no clear, consistent political orientation, then the level of internal migration is not likely to have much effect. However, if a state draws its internal migrants primarily from conservative or liberal states, then internal migration is likely to play a role in changing state political outcomes, and this effect should grow in magnitude as the level of internal migration grows. Similar to Robinson and Noriega's argument, the expectation here is that the impact of internal migration is a function of both the level of internal migration and the political context of the states from which those migrants come.

While there are differences in sources of internal migrants across states, some states do stand out as primary sources. As might be expected with any measure based on population, large states lead the way. However, the leading sources of internal migrants tend overall to be centrist or liberal, and competitive or Democratic states. New York leads the way, with 6.1% of citizen voting-age internal migrants claiming it as their birth state, followed by California (5.1%), Illinois (3.6%), Pennsylvania (3.3%), Ohio (2.9%), Texas (2.8%), Michigan (2.4%), and New Jersey (2.2%). Given that these states are overall more Democratic than the rest of the country, it is interesting that there is no relationship between internal migrant population and change in presidential votes. One potential explanation is that the Democratic advantage in these states is much greater now (the Democratic share of two-party vote ran about 8 points higher in these states than in the remaining states from 2004 to 2012) than it was when most of the internal migrants were born and raised in those states (only a 2-point difference from 1972 to 1980). This suggests that it is important to rely on historical patterns of political tendencies when trying to account for the impact of migration over the long haul. If we were focused on short-term migration—Where did the migrants live five years ago?—then capturing the current political environment of the states would make more sense.[5]

In addition, while the eight states listed above are the leading sources of internal migrants, some states draw very heavily from them, while other states draw very few migrants from them. In fact each state has its own set of source states from which it tends to draw the greatest share of internal migrants. To get a sense of these differences and how they can affect political change in the states, consider the experiences of Ohio, Vermont, and Wyoming. In Ohio 24.6% of the CVAP are internal migrants, and the leading sources for this population flow are (in order of magnitude) Pennsylvania, West Virginia, Kentucky, Michigan, and New York. These five states combine to account for 46% of Ohio's internal migrant population. Given the relatively diverse political background of these states, it is no surprise that Ohio has moved very little politically over the past several decades. Vermont's experience differs from Ohio's in two important ways. First, half of Vermont's CVAP was born in another state, increasing the likelihood that the internal migrant population could have a more profound impact on the movement in Vermont's political profile. Second, the leading sources of Vermont's internal migrant population—New York, Massachusetts, New Hampshire, Connecticut, and New Jersey (in order of magnitude)—are Democratic and liberal, with the exception of New Hampshire, and constitute 65% of Vermont's internal migrants. Finally, consider Wyoming's experience: 61% of that state's CVAP are internal migrants; the leading sources of this migration are (in order of magnitude) Colorado, California, Utah, Nebraska, and South Dakota; and these states together account for 38% of Wyoming's internal migrant population. With the exception of California, these source states historically are relatively Republican and relatively conservative. Given the differences in scope and sources, we might expect internal migration to affect these states differently. Wyoming, with a large internal migrant population drawn from fairly conservative states, should move toward the Republican Party; Ohio, with a small proportion of its population being internal migrants drawn from a politically heterogeneous set of states, may not be affected very much; and Vermont, with about half of its population born in states that are more liberal than the rest of the country, should be moved in the Democratic direction. This is exactly what has happened in all three states (see Figure 1.5).

Internal migrants beyond those coming from the top five source states influence each of these states, so it is important to gauge the impact of internal migration on each state by taking into account the overall contributions of each of the forty-nine other states and their political leanings. I use estimates of state political ideology of each source state and weight those contexts by the proportion of the population in a given state coming from each source state.[6] One tricky aspect of this measure is the need to capture state ideology not at the current time period but at some period in the past that reflects the political tenor of the birth state when internal migrants were likely to be socialized and become involved in the political process and hence is likely to reflect the predispositions of internal migrants. We don't know when internal migrants left their birth state, so we have to use some measure of birth state context, accepting that it is a rough estimate of how the birth state milieu of internal migrants influences changes in state politics. The average age for internal migrants in 2012 was fifty, which means the first election for the average internal migrant was in 1980. Using this as a reference point, the net ideology (% liberal minus % conservative) of each state, averaged for 1972–80, is used to estimate birth state ideological context, which is assumed to represent something like the expected ideological influence of migration streams coming from each migrant source state.

The method for calculating the weighted birth state ideology (WBI_i) is presented in Equation 3.1, where ρ_{ij} is the proportion of the CVAP in state i that was born in state j, and ID_j is the net liberal advantage (liberal minus conservative identifiers) in state j from 1972–80.

$$WBI_i = \sum_{j=1}^{n}(\rho_{i,j} * ID_j) \tag{3.1}$$

This measure takes into account both the magnitude and political context of internal migration: high values indicate, on balance, greater liberal influence from internal migration, and low values indicate greater conservative influence, while a value of zero indicates a wash.

When this measure is calculated for Ohio, Vermont, and Wyoming, the resulting values make sense given the primary sources for internal migrants in each of these states. For Wyoming, a state that drew heavily from Mountain West and midwestern states, the overall value of the weighted internal migrant ideology variable was –.56, indicating, on balance, a conservative influence from internal migration. (The mean value for this variable across all fifty states is .49, indicating a somewhat liberal influence from migration.) For Ohio, a state with a more heterogeneous internal migration stream, the weighted internal migrant ideology variable was –.04, somewhat more conservative than the overall average but very close to a wash. For Vermont, a state that draws its internal migrant population heavily from the northeastern United States, the weighted ideology value was 2.50, indicating a very liberal influence from internal migration.

This measure of the potential political impact of internal migration rests upon the assumption that migrating voters reflect the political tenor of the states in which they were born. This is not to say that every migrant born in Massachusetts, for instance, is a liberal Democrat, or that every internal migrant born in Utah is a conservative Republican, but on average people from Massachusetts will be more liberal and Democratic than people from Utah. As Robinson and Noriega (2010) point out, there is not a lot of evidence that people who migrate from a given state are substantially different in political views than people who stay in that state. This is the perspective I take, that, generally speaking, people who were born in (and presumably spent some time in) liberal states are, on average, more liberal than people born in conservative states. When those people move, they bring their political perspective with them and have an impact on the politics of their destination state, especially if migration patterns are consistently liberal or conservative and of significant magnitude.

Ideally we could test this idea by identifying the birth state of survey respondents who are internal migrants and then assess the extent to which their political views reflect the state where they were born. Unfortunately one of the primary sources of data on public opinion and elections, the American National Election Study (ANES), has not recorded birth state information since the early 1990s, and the General Social Survey (GSS) does not identify state of birth or current state of residence due to privacy concerns. However, both the ANES and the GSS ask respondents questions that allow us to identify where they spent part of their childhood. The GSS has a series of items about residential mobility since the age of sixteen, including one that identifies which of the nine census regions respondents lived in when they were sixteen.[7] This variable can be matched with the region in which respondents currently live in order to identify those respondents who are *regional migrants*, having moved between regions since their teen years. While the ANES data do identify the state in which respondents grew up, the samples for most states are quite small, so I aggregated these responses by the same census regions used for the GSS data. This regional focus is a bit different from the way internal migrants are treated in the rest of this chapter, but it does give us our best opportunity to see if, on average, internal migrants reflect the politics of the place from which they come.

The following analysis is limited to internal regional migrants. For the GSS this is native-born respondents who currently live in a region that is different from where they lived when they were sixteen, utilizing the 2008–12 GSS surveys. For the ANES this is native-born respondents living in a region that is different from where they say they grew up, utilizing the 2000–2008 ANES studies.[8] Current ideological leanings of these respondents are measured using questions that asked respondents to place themselves on a 7-point scale, ranging from extremely liberal to extremely conservative. This question was then recoded into two dichotomous variables, one identifying respondents who provided a "liberal" response and one identifying respondents who provided a "conservative" response. These dichotomous variables were then aggregated by region, using the region in which the respondents lived when they were children. From this we can get the net ideology of internal regional migrants by childhood region. We can correlate this aggregated measure with the overall ideological leanings of those regions from 1972 to 1980, using the net liberal advantage measure that was used to create the measure of weighted home state ideology in Equation 3.1. If internal migrants, on average, reflect the politics of the place from which they came, a historical measure of regional ideology should be related to the average ideology of contemporary survey respondents who lived in those regions during their childhood.

This relationship is explored in Figure 3.3, where the top graph presents the relationship for GSS respondents and the bottom graph for ANES respondents. The horizontal axis is the historical net ideology (liberal minus conservative) averaged across states within each of the nine census regions. The vertical axis represents the net ideology averaged across survey respondents from within the same census regions, except that here *region* represents the region in which the respondents spent part of their childhood. These averages are restricted only to those respondents who live in a region different from the one in which they grew up (ANES) or lived when they were sixteen years old (GSS). This group represents 21%

of all respondents for both the GSS and ANES samples, yielding 1,140 respondents for the GSS and 1,003 for the ANES. The relationships are quite striking. Beginning with the GSS data, the mean ideological predisposition of internal regional migrants from 2008 to 2012 is very closely tied to the historical (1972–80) measure of regional ideological predisposition for the regions they lived in when they were sixteen (r = .82). A very similar pattern is found for ANES data, where the correlation between average current ideological orientation of region migrants from 2000 to 2008 and the historical measure of the ideology of region in which they grew up is .79.[9] These findings do not necessarily say anything about individual regional migrants but instead speak to the overall outlook of the group. Regional migrants, on average, reflect the political leanings of the regions from which they migrated.

The patterns presented in Figure 3.3 certainly provide support for the expectation that migration from one state to another is likely to bear the imprint of the source state's politics. If source states are consistently of one political stripe or another, and if the level of migration is of sufficient magnitude, then we should expect to see change in the destination state's political orientation. Returning to Figure 3.2, we see the relationship between the weighted home-state liberalism of internal migrants and change in support for Democratic candidates presented in the lower right panel. This is a relatively strong relationship, with Democratic vote increasing as the birth state liberalism of internal migrants increases (r = .63). Similar to the relationship for foreign-born migrants, there is a curvilinear trend to the data: when there is relatively little bias to the home-state liberalism for internal migrants (only slightly liberal or slightly conservative), there is a lot of diversity in political changes—some states saw steep Democratic gains, while other states saw steep Democratic losses—but as the political tenor of internal migration grows more liberal, Democrats make substantial gains. Also similar to the pattern for foreign-born migrants, the lower right quadrant of the figure is completely empty, meaning that there are no cases of relatively high levels of internal migrant home-state liberalism and Democratic decline during this time period. It is also interesting to note that there are no states in which the political tendencies of

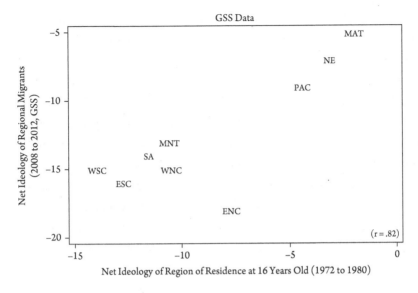

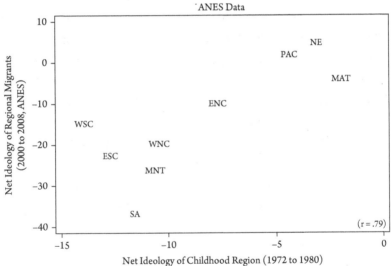

Figure 3.3 The Relationship between the Ideological Disposition of Migrants' Childhood Region of Residence and the Contemporary Ideological Disposition of Those Regional Migrants

NOTE: ENC = East North Central, ESC = East South Central, MAT = Mid-Atlantic, MNT = Mountain, NE = New England, PAC = Pacific, SA = South Atlantic, WNC = West North Central, WSC = West South Central. See text for description of independent and dependent variables.

internal migrant source states are strongly conservative, perhaps reflecting the fact that the leading sources of internal migration tend to be large, Democratic states. This figure drives home an important point: it is unreasonable to expect a substantively strong or interesting relationship between internal migration and political change without considering the political context of the states from which the migrants came. Once that context is accounted for, internal migration emerges as a potentially important source of political change in the states.

It is interesting that the weighted ideology of internal migration and foreign-born migration do not overlap very much as explanations. Overall the correlation between the percentage of foreign-born and the weighted home-state liberalism for internal migrants is just .35. A visual examination of the two scatter plots (bottom two panels in Figure 3.2) clarifies this, at least in terms of data points that are significantly off-trend, and helps illustrate the extent to which the two sources of migration may be complementary rather than competing explanations. Some states that are not well explained by foreign-born migration, such as Maine, New Hampshire, Texas, and Vermont, fit the pattern for home-state liberalism much better, and a number of states that are not particularly well explained by internal migrant home-state liberalism, such as California, Hawaii, Illinois, and New York, are more easily accounted for by the pattern of foreign-born migration.

The combined and relative impact of foreign-born and internal migration on changes in party support is assessed in Table 3.3, utilizing a multiple regression model.[10] Both variables are significantly and positively related to changes in party support over time, and the relative effects of the two variables (standardized coefficients) are very similar in magnitude.[11] One way to get a sense of the potential impact of these two variables is to estimate outcomes that would be expected to occur for different values of percentage of foreign-born and weighted home-state ideology. Given that the two independent variables are measured on different scales, the coefficients are a bit difficult to compare. The standardized coefficients are useful in this respect. The coefficients in the farthest right column address this issue by expressing how the dependent variable is expected

Table 3.3 THE IMPACT OF IMMIGRATION STREAMS ON CHANGES IN PARTY
SUPPORT AT THE STATE LEVEL IN PRESIDENTIAL ELECTIONS FROM 1972–80
TO 2004–12

	b/s.e.	ΔY, S$_x$
Weighted Home-State Liberalism	*3.169*	3.1
	.646	
Percentage of Foreign-Born	*.718*	3.3
	.141	
Constant	*−4.969*	—
	.969	
N	50	
Adj. R²	.59	
RMSE	4.231	

NOTE: The dependent variable is change in estimated Democratic support from
1972–80 to 2004–12, based on the trend in the Democratic share of the two-party
vote, centered around the national two-party division (see Figures 1.3 and 1.4).
Weighted home-state liberalism is measured in 2008, using Equation 3.1, and
percentage of foreign-born is measured in 2008. Both independent variables are
based on the CVAP. b/s.e. = slope/standard error; ΔY, S$_x$ = change in the dependent
variable for a standard deviation change in the independent variable. **Bold** = p < .05;
bold italics = p < .01 (one-tailed).

to change in response to a standard deviation change in the value of the
independent variables. The values of these standardized coefficients show
both variables to be of roughly equal magnitude: a standard deviation
increase (decrease) in either independent variable generates approximately a 3-point increase (decrease) in the Democratic share of the centered two-party vote.

It is important to understand that at least part of the effect of migration reflects the changes in state population characteristics that flow from
migration patterns. Many of the patterns found in the national survey
data in Table 3.2 are manifested at the state level as well. Foreign-born as
a percentage of the CVAP is fairly strongly related to change in the percentage of the population who have an advanced degree (r = .43), whose
occupation is classified as professional (r = .46), and who are nonwhite

(r = .84). Internal migration (weighted by birth-state ideology) is also related to important changes in state characteristics, including change in percentage with an advanced degree (r = .67), percentage with a professional occupation (r = .44), and change in net Democratic identification and net liberal identification (r = .53 and .58, respectively). This is not to say that migration patterns produced all of these changes in state characteristics, for it is possible that the state contexts created by these demographic and political factors made some states more or less attractive destinations for certain types of migrants. In-migration of both foreign-born and internal migrants is, however, a likely contributing source of change in state demographic and political characteristics, as well as change in electoral support.

SUMMARY

Population migration is a potentially important source of demographic and political change in the states. But not all states are affected equally by migration. Some experience high levels of migration, with upward of 60% of their population born somewhere else. These tend to be mostly small states that have experienced rapid population growth over the past forty years. Here Nevada leads the way, with more than 80% of its CVAP born elsewhere. At the same time, a number of states—mostly those with low population growth—have relatively few (less than 30%) residents born elsewhere. These differences in levels of migration set the stage for differences in the impact of migration on state politics. But differences in magnitude are not enough to determine how migration might affect change in the states.

As it turns out, the source of migration is as important as the volume of migration. When considering only the size of the migrant population, there is a relatively modest positive relationship between migration and change in Democratic presidential votes. This sort of broad treatment of migration ignores the fact that migrants are a heterogeneous group and that many of the politically important differences among migrants can be connected to the places from which they came. First, the foreign-born population stands out as substantially different from internal migrants along important demographic and political dimensions, especially race and ethnicity, party affiliation, and political ideology. Perhaps most important for studies of political change, these differences are much more stark today than they were forty years ago. Separating the foreign-born population from internal migrants is illuminating: states with a large foreign-born population almost uniformly have large increases in support for Democratic presidential candidates. This points to an important tie-in to contemporary political debates over immigration: although there are no doubt many principled reasons why most Republican presidential candidates favor relatively strict immigration policies and most Democratic presidential candidates favor policies that include a "pathway to citizenship," it bears pointing out that there are real political consequences to changes in the foreign-born citizen population. Relatively lenient policies that facilitate immigration and eventual citizenship are likely to result in increases in a block of voters who are much more inclined to support Democratic than Republican candidates.

It is also important not to treat internal migrants as a homogeneous monolith. When focusing just on levels of internal migration, there is no discernible difference in political outcomes between states with high and low levels. This is because states do not draw their internal migrant populations equally from the same types of states. In some states internal migrants tend to come from states that are, on balance, relatively conservative, pushing the state in a conservative direction. In other states the sources of internal migrants might be relatively liberal and push the state in a liberal direction. And in yet other states the sources of internal migrants could be politically heterogeneous and have very little net effect on state politics. Importantly the impact of internal migration is likely to be greatest when the source states are relatively liberal or conservative and the internal migrant population is substantial, relative to the state native population. When the liberalism of the birth states of internal migrants is weighted by the size of the internal migrant population, there is a strong positive relationship between internal migration and change in Democratic support over time.

Migration patterns are an important part of the explanation of changes in state patterns of presidential support. Their importance derives not just from the direct effects shown in this chapter but also from the fact that migration can be connected to broader patterns of changes in the demographic and political makeup of state electorates, changes that contribute to a fuller account of the transformation of the geographic bases of party support in presidential elections.

Compositional Change and Political Change

Most accounts of changing geographic patterns of political support include references to the changing demography of state electorates. Although many Republicans focus explicitly on changes in the racial and ethnic makeup of key states (Gluek 2014; Ladd 2014; Murphy and Wisecup 2013), others have focused on other potential sources of change, including changes in the size of the well-educated professional class (Hood and McKee 2010; Judis and Teixeira 2004; Manza and Brooks 1999) and migration patterns (Bishop 2009; Gimpel and Schuknecht 2001; Jurjevich and Plane 2012; Robinson and Noriega 2010). There are many ways to slice the demographic pie—many more than just race, ethnicity, and place of origin—and many of the pieces overlap significantly with each other. The goal of this chapter is to wade through the many conceptualizations of how group membership is likely to affect political support, offer some individual-level evidence from the 2012 election, and put together a parsimonious model in which changes in party support at the state level are explained by changes in key state demographic characteristics.

GROUPS AND PARTY SUPPORT

The idea of a group basis for voting behavior has always played an important role in studies of U.S. elections. Two foundational studies of modern electoral studies were among the first to identify and quantify the group basis of voting behavior and public opinion. These studies— Lazarsfeld et al.'s (1944) *The People's Choice* and Berelson et al.'s (1954) *Voting*—are often referred to as representing the Columbia school of electoral studies, based on the authors' affiliations with Columbia University. Both studies used relatively elaborate panel survey designs to analyze voter decision making during campaigns, Lazarsfeld et al. in Erie County, Ohio, during the 1940 presidential election, and Berelson et al. in Elmira, New York, during the 1948 election. In the end, however, it turned out that exposure to campaign events and discussions had little impact on voters. Instead Lazarsfeld et al. uncovered a social group dimension to the vote—religious, class, and geographic identities lined up squarely behind the parties—that was so strong that whatever individual-level movement in vote intention there was during the campaign tended mostly to be from misplaced voters returning to vote with their dominant social group. This pattern of group-based voting led to the creation of the Index of Political Predisposition (IPP), on which voters were scaled according to the Republican or Democratic predispositions of their social groups. The strength of the empirical connection between the IPP and votes was so strong that Lazarsfeld et al. (1944, 27) concluded, "A person thinks politically as he is socially. Social characteristics determine political preferences." Berelson et al. (1954) found much the same process at work in the 1948 election: very few people changed their vote intention during the campaign, and those who did tended to fall in line with the voting patterns of their social group.

The group basis for vote choice continued to play an important part in the development of voting studies, assuming the role of antecedent factor in the development of the concept of party identification in *The American Voter* (Campbell et al. 1960; Miller and Shanks 1996) and also assuming a prominent role in many conceptions of political realignment (Key 1959; Mayhew 2002; Petrocik 1981; Pomper 1967).[1]

Before examining some of the important group-based voting cleavages that have generated attention in American politics, it is useful to reiterate the theoretical connection among groups, parties, and candidates. As described in chapter 2, some group connections make a great deal of sense based on a material or "benefits" perspective: groups align with parties that pursue policies that have some direct, tangible benefit to the group. Racial, occupational, and class cleavages can be understood in this context, to some extent. Racial minorities, union members, and low-income voters could reasonably see a more direct connection between their interests and the success of the Democratic Party. Higher income voters and business people should have an easy time connecting their interests to the Republican Party. But interests are only part of the story. Some groups are not tied to parties so much by shared, tangible interests as they are by shared preferences; for these groups the connection to political parties may be based as much or more on preference as on interests (Petrocik 1981). Consider, for example, the connection between religiosity and party support, whereby support for the Republican Party is strongly and positively related to indicators of religious commitment (Olson and Green 2006). It is not so much the case that the deeply religious derive clear, tangible benefits from Republican policies; rather the Republican Party, more than the Democratic Party, supports a traditional and conservative social agenda that dovetails nicely with the preferences of deeply religious voters (Bishop 2009; Olson and Green 2006). Similarly, as pointed out in chapter 2, it is difficult to imagine that the Democratic Party provides direct tangible benefits to voters with advanced degrees who, after all, tend to be white, are unlikely to belong to unions, and have relatively high levels of income. Instead the appeal of the Democratic Party for the highly educated and professional class is more likely to stem from shared ideological perspectives, especially on social and postmaterial issues, such as gay rights, reproductive issues, and environmentalism (Feldman and Johnston 2014; Houtman 2001; Kahn 2002).

Most of my analysis of group-based change in the states comes from the study of aggregate data on group size in the states. However, the vast majority of group-based analysis of voting behavior comes from individual-level studies in which the demographic characteristics of survey respondents are correlated with their vote choice, producing evidence of gaps in group preferences (Green and Olson 2009). Before moving on to the core of the aggregate analysis, I review some of the existing evidence of group-based voting, using survey data from the 2012 election to illustrate the utility of those gaps as potential explanations of contemporary voting patterns.

Race and Ethnicity

Historically one of the largest gaps in voting behavior occurs along racial and ethnic lines. Although the contemporary focus is on differences in voting behavior between whites and nonwhites at the presidential level, the idea of racial or ethnic political solidarity is not new to American politics and historically has even encompassed ethnic divides within the white community (Lorinskas et al. 1969; Pomper 1966). The most notable change in the dynamics of racial alignment is reflected in the gulf between white and black voters, which grew in magnitude beginning in the mid-1960s in the wake of Democratic support for civil rights, the Goldwater candidacy, and the Republican embrace of the "southern strategy" (Black and Black 2009; Carmines and Stimson 1989; McClerking 2009). However, black voters were not alone in moving toward the Democratic Party. The Latino vote has also moved somewhat steadily to the Democratic column, and the increased size and cohesion of this group is of significant enough magnitude that it has become pivotal in several states, perhaps providing the margin necessary for Democrats to win at the national level (Barreto et al. 2010). The source of Latino support for the Democratic Party likely stems from the overall level of liberal attitudes of Latinos (Segura 2012) and from Democratic appeals on issues related to immigration policy (Collingwood et al. 2014). In addition, though less work has been done on Asian American political attitudes, recent elections have seen steep increases in support for Democratic candidates among Asian Americans and Pacific Islanders (Ramakrishnan 2014, 2015).

Socioeconomic Status

One of the earliest identified voting cleavages was social class, with blue-collar, unionized, and low-income voters throwing their support behind Democratic candidates, and white-collar and high-income voters supporting Republican candidates (Berelson et al. 1954; Campbell et al. 1960; Lazarsfeld et al. 1944). The relationship between socioeconomic status and party support has changed substantially and is not nearly as strong or linear as it once was (Brewer and Stonecash 2006; Manza and Brooks 1999; Ortiz and Stonecash 2009). Among other factors that have altered this relationship is the fact that many socioeconomic variables are also related to overall levels of cultural conservatism, with low-income and low-education voters tending to be culturally conservative, and high-income voters holding moderate to liberal social views. This tends to cross-pressure socially conservative low-income voters, whose loyalty to the Democratic Party can erode as a result, as well as high-income voters, who hold more liberal views on social issues and whose support for the Republican Party can erode as well (Ortiz and Stonecash 2009). In fact Ortiz and Stonecash maintain that the increasingly constrained relationship between income and vote choice may end up as a net loss to the Republican Party; they argue that the changing relationship "has not occurred because Republicans have been able to attract the less affluent, but because they are alienating the more affluent."

This finding ties in nicely with research on occupational status and vote choice. As discussed earlier, one of the key findings in this area is that the once very Republican professional class has moved significantly in the direction of the Democratic Party over time (Brooks and Manza 1997a, b; Hout et al. 1999; Judis and Teixeira 2004; Manza and Brooks 1999). Manza and Brooks offer two different explanations of this change: that the professional class is increasingly made up of public employees and people who work in the nonprofit sector and therefore have a vested interest in

Democratic success, or the professional class has become increasingly liberal on social issues. Manza and Brooks find that increased social liberalism among professionals provides the best empirical explanation. This fits nicely with the suggestion that increased attention to cultural issues on the part of political elites has helped activate ideology and moved professionals toward the Democratic Party (Judis and Teixeira 2004). One aspect of professionals that helps explain this pattern is that they have a high level of education compared to other occupational groups. While high level of education tends to be connected to greater economic conservatism, it is also true that the highly educated tend to be relatively liberal on social issues (Feldman and Johnston 2014; Houtman 2001) and on issues such as environmental regulation (Kahn 2002).

The Gender Gap

If the racial gap stands out as one of the most profound gaps in terms of magnitude, the gender gap surely stands out in terms of the attention it gets. Often hailed as decisive by political commentators (Kornacki 2012), the gender gap in voting has ranged in magnitude (female percentage voting Democratic minus male percentage voting Democratic) from 4 to 11 points in presidential elections from 1980 to 2012.[2] Like the relationship between race and vote choice, the nature of the gender gap has evolved over time. Kaufmann and Petrocik (1999) were among the first to track the dynamics of the gender gap, finding that women were actually slightly more Republican than men (in both voting patterns and party identification) in the 1950s and early 1960s, but that the gap was reversed and grew throughout the subsequent decades. Notably the gap is not a result of women flocking to the Democratic Party but of men increasingly embracing the Republican Party over time (Box-Steffensmeier et al. 2004; Kaufmann and Petrocik 1999). Despite conventional wisdom that the gender gap is the result of differences of opinion on "women's" issues, such as abortion, there have not been substantial changes in the opinion gaps between men and women across these and other issues (Kaufmann 2009). Instead the primary explanation for the emergence and continuation of the gender gap is changes in the emphasis men and women attach to groups of issues; with increasing numbers of single women in the electorate, as well as changes in the traditional family structure (Box-Steffensmeier et al. 2004), social welfare and cultural issues (reproductive rights, gay rights, women's equality) have emerged as prominent sources of the gender gap (Kaufmann 2002, 2009).[3]

Religion

Religion also plays an important role in shaping party identification and voting behavior, though our understanding of this relationship has changed over time. Religious denomination used to help define the social basis for party support; Catholics traditionally were strong supporters of the Democratic Party and Protestants were strong supporters of the Republican Party (Berelson et al. 1954; Campbell et al. 1960; Lazarsfeld et al. 1944). Today, however, religious denomination is not viewed as nearly as important as the strength of religious commitment (Leege and Kellstedt 1993; Olson and Green 2006). Although measures of religious commitment vary across studies, one measure that is commonly used is frequency of attendance at religious services, and those who attend frequently are much more likely to vote Republican than those who attend less frequently or not at all. Part of the explanation for this relationship is that regular attenders are generally more conservative, more traditional, and place more emphasis on "moral" issues than do infrequent attenders (Olson and Green 2006). It is generally assumed that this relationship grew stronger in the 1980s and 1990s due to the Republican Party's courtship of political elites in the Christian conservative movement (Bishop 2009; Judis and Teixeira 2004; Milkis et al. 2013). A rival hypothesis is that religious conservatives were pushed to the Republican Party by the "irreverent left," although some evidence suggests that any hostility toward religion by the Left was a result of religious alignment rather than a cause (Pieper 2011).

Marital Status

The potential list of demographic characteristics is almost endless, and there is no good reason to simply segment demography in any way possible looking for influences on vote choice. However, one other potentially important voting gap is the marriage gap. Evidence of a marriage gap first emerged in the 1972 election (Weisberg 1987) and has persisted over time, growing in magnitude over the past several election cycles (Gerskoff 2009). Findings in this area of research show that married people have a substantially higher probability of voting for the Republican candidate than do unmarried people (Gerskoff 2009; Plutzer and McBurnett 1991; Weisberg 1987). In some analyses this pattern persists even when controlling for variables that might explain the gap (Plutzer and McBurnett 1991). While the precise source of the marriage gap remains elusive, Gerskoff (2009) offers three potential explanations: financial insecurity (unmarried people are more likely to be financially insecure and hence could be attracted to the Democratic Party based on its traditional support for programs aimed at helping the poor); values (marriage is a traditional institution, a choice people make, and people who are married are more likely to be culturally conservative and find Republican cultural appeals attractive); and mobilization (Democrats are more likely to reach out to single voters, and Republicans are more likely to reach out to married voters). The values-based explanation offers interesting possibilities, especially for examining changes in the relationship between marital status and vote over time, as the parties diverged on social and cultural issues.

DEMOGRAPHICS AND THE 2012 PRESIDENTIAL ELECTION

Data from the 2012 presidential election provide insights into the relative importance of a set of demographic characteristics on vote choice. The web-based module of the American National Election Study is used to demonstrate the effects of many of the variables just discussed.[4] These effects are summarized in Figure 4.1. The probability of voting for the Democratic incumbent, Barack Obama, is estimated for people with discrete demographic characteristics, using logistic regression. These are simple estimates, representing the effects of each category of characteristics without controlling for overlapping group memberships. Perhaps the starkest differences in party support occur along racial and ethnic lines. Support for Obama ranges from a low of .44 among non-Latino white respondents to .56 among non-Latino "other" racial and ethnic groups (this includes Native Americans, Asian Americans, and others who are neither Latino nor black), .71 among Latino respondents, and .96 among black respondents. This pattern of differences is statistically significant (chi-square = 90.31, p = .00) and substantively important and is very much in keeping with findings from recent elections (McClerking 2009). As demonstrated in chapter 3, migrant status is also tied to race and ethnicity; the relationship between the size of the foreign-born population and changes in Democratic support shown earlier is supported in this figure, where we see that foreign-born respondents were about 15 points more likely to vote Democratic than native-born respondents (chi-square = 8.86, p = .003).

The results for indicators of socioeconomic status generally comport with expectations, with a few wrinkles. Income (chi-square = 42.36, p = .000), occupation (chi-square = 12.65, p = .006), and education (chi-square = 21.12, p=.009) are all significantly related to vote choice. President Obama enjoyed his highest vote margin among those with relatively low and high incomes, those with the lowest and highest levels of education, and those with a professional occupation; he received the least support from middle-income groups, middle-education groups, and people in management occupations.[5] Interestingly there are no clear differences between union and nonunion voters in the 2012 ANES survey data (chi-square = 1.26, p = .262). This finding is significantly at odds with previous decades of ANES surveys, though exit poll surveys show some drop-off in union voting beginning in 2004.[6]

The gender gap also appears to have been alive and well during the 2012 election, with female voters somewhat more likely (.08) than male voters

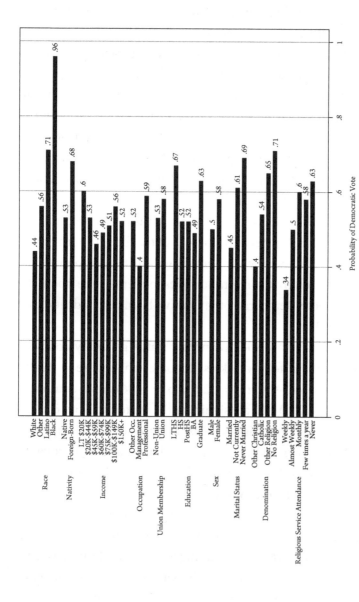

Figure 4.1 Demographic Characteristics and Presidential Vote Choice in 2012

NOTE: All entries are the estimated probability of voting for Obama in 2012 for each group characteristic, based on simple logistic regressions, with dichotomous independent variables representing individual group characteristics. Because the measure of occupational status used here was not available for the face-to-face sample, data from the web-based sample of the 2012 ANES were used to estimate the probabilities. Web-based weights were used in all analyses.

to vote Democratic. This effect is relatively small in comparison to many others in Figure 4.1 but is statistically significant (chi-square = 10.02, p = .002) and is on par with recent gender gaps. The marital gap also shows a fairly pronounced division, with single respondents (defined as those who have never been married) about 24 points more likely to vote Democratic than those who are currently married, and about 8 points more likely than those who had been but are no longer married (chi-square = 37.58, p = .000).

Both religious affiliation and frequency of religious service attendance have important effects on vote choice. Respondents who report weekly attendance at religious services have a .34 probability of voting Democratic, while those who never attend religious services have a .63 probability. The pattern of support across attendance categories in not perfectly monotonic, but the group differences are very strong (chi-square = 87.14, p = .000). Patterns of religious affiliation fit with expectations from previous research: non-Catholic Christians are the least likely to vote Democratic, followed by Catholics, then "other" religions, and "not religious" (chi-square = 103.04, p = .000).[7] The differences across affiliation groups may overstate the relationship a bit, since only 2.5% of the sample affiliated with a non-Christian ("other") religion. Affiliation and attendance patterns overlap a bit (Cramer's V = .35), with non-Catholic Christians most likely to attend religious services, followed by Catholics, then other religions, and "not religious."

All in all, the patterns in Figure 4.1 reflect expectations from previous research. As noted, however, many of these variables overlap significantly with other variables. For example, race and ethnicity overlap with religious affiliation, religious attendance, and all measures of socioeconomic status; income, education, and occupation overlap with each other. This begs the question of which characteristics remain significantly related to vote choice when controlling for all other characteristics. When all variables are entered into a single model, many of the patterns presented in Figure 4.1 emerge again, though all of the relationships are weaker and a couple of them are no longer significant. The most substantial changes are among socioeconomic indicators: income differences are no longer statistically significant as a group; education is still significant as a group, but this is driven by advanced-degree recipients, who stand out as significantly different from all groups other than those without a high school diploma; and occupational status is also significant as a group, though there is no significant difference between management and "other" occupations, while professionals stand out as giving significantly more support to Obama than either of the other two occupation categories. Interestingly nativity loses significance in the combined model, and union household becomes significant, though the probability of voting for Obama is only .06 greater for people living in union households.

The relationships presented in Figure 4.1 represent a set of demographic characteristics typically included when estimating models of vote choice. It is possible to partition demography into even finer distinctions (white males, single females, white Protestants, etc.); however, the point here is not to account for every possible permutation but to illustrate how people with different characteristics often line up behind different parties and candidates.

MOVING TO AGGREGATE PATTERNS

This evidence is illustrative and helps build the case for examining compositional changes in the states as a determinant of changes in patterns of presidential support at the state level. However, the data presented in Figure 4.1 are based on individuals at one point in time, and it is important to bear in mind that the process of aggregation, or confounding relationships with other variables, could lead to different patterns at the aggregate level. This is typically a greater concern when trying to make inferences about individuals based on aggregate patterns (Robinson 1950), but it is also sometimes the case that relationships found at the individual level are not manifested, or even present perverse findings, in aggregate analyses. Perhaps one of the best-known examples of this is found in the relationship between income level and voting behavior. While it is common to find that Democrats enjoy their highest level of support among lower-income voters, the exact opposite is true at the state level: Democrats typically fare best in the relatively wealthy New England and Mid-Atlantic states and fare worst in the relatively poor states of the South and Plains. This paradox is explored in fine detail by Gelman et al. (2008), who find that the phenomenon is fairly recent, perhaps due in part to the combined effects of the emergence of cultural and social issues and the tendency for poor internal migrants, who are generally socially conservative, to move to "Red" states, and wealthy internal migrants, who are generally socially liberal, to move to "Blue" states.

My own sense is that this type of problem is more likely to affect findings in static research designs in which the focus is on *levels* of variables rather than *changes* in the values of variables. The remainder of this chapter focuses on *changes* over time in the levels of key demographic and political variables, aggregated at the state level. Intuitively this is different from looking at levels of the independent and dependent variables at a fixed point in time. Consider race, for example. We know from Figure 4.1 that nonwhite voters overwhelmingly support the Democratic Party. However, we also know that states in the conservative South have relatively high concentrations of nonwhite voters,[8] which leads to fairly weak or, in some cases, perverse cross-sectional correlations between the percentages of nonwhite and Democratic vote share in any given year. Because this and other variables examined in this chapter are expressed in terms of increases or decreases over time, the hypothesis is not that Democrats should do better in states with a substantial nonwhite population than in other states at any given point in time but that—regardless of the historical size of the nonwhite population—Democrats should see their vote share increase more in states that have seen the greatest increases over time in their nonwhite population than in other states. This does not mean Democrats are expected to win in states with substantial increases in nonwhite populations, just that they should improve their margin more in those states than in states with smaller increases.

Note that this discussion is couched in terms of changes in *relative* standing over time. This is because for many of the variables considered here, there are strong secular trends over time such that all states move in the same direction, so we may see gains (or losses) in every state. For instance, from the early 1970s to 2012 all states saw a decline in the percentage of their white population. Some states saw relatively steep declines, while others saw relatively modest declines. But we don't expect to see Democratic gains in all states just because all states lost white population. Instead the expectation is that Democratic gains (Republican losses) should be greatest in states with steep declines in white population, and Democratic losses (Republican gains) should be the greatest in states with the slightest declines. In effect, when measuring change in population characteristics over time we are measuring changes in the relative levels over time, since all states are measured at the same points in time.[9]

AGGREGATE PATTERNS OF CHANGE

I contrast aggregate patterns of changes in key demographic and political characteristics with changes in state-level election outcomes to gain a simple, bivariate impression of how changes in state characteristics are related to changes in support for the parties in presidential elections. My strategy is similar to that used in my analysis of migration effects in chapter 3: change in average estimated centered Democratic vote from 1972–80 to 2004–12 is the dependent variable, and change in state characteristics during the same time periods is the independent variable. It bears repeating that the change in vote measure is based on the trend in party support, estimated in Figures 1.3 and 1.4, which provides a measure of candidate support purged of home-state effects as well as the southern region effects particular to the Carter and Clinton candidacies.

Race and Ethnicity

As noted earlier, changes in the racial and ethnic composition of the states are frequently cited as an important source of political change, with a primary focus on the increased size of the minority (nonwhite) population in key states (Gluek 2014; Judis and Teixeira 2004; Murphy and Wisecup

2013). My approach is to examine the overall relationship between change in the nonwhite CVAP and change in party support, and then examine changes in the separate components of the nonwhite CVAP—changes in the percentage of Latino, the percentage of non-Latino black, and the percentage of non-Latino other (mostly Native American and Asian and Pacific Islander). These relationships are presented in Figure 4.2, where the joint outcome of change in population characteristic and change in votes for each state is represented by the state abbreviation, and the solid line is a bivariate regression slope that summarizes the linear trend in the data. The upper left cell shows the relationship between changes in the nonwhite population and changes in votes. As mentioned earlier, there are no states in which the nonwhite population decreased during this time period: the average increase across all states was 8 percentage points, ranging from a low of 1.6 points in West Virginia to a high of 25.1 points in California. There is a general trend in the data toward increasing Democratic vote share in response to increases in the nonwhite population (r =.43). Generally speaking, states with the greatest increases in the nonwhite population are also states with relatively large swings toward the Democratic Party. On average Democrats gained 4.49 points in states with above-average gains in their nonwhite population and lost 2.15 points in states with below-average growth in the nonwhite population. States that fit this pattern most clearly are California, Florida, Maryland, New Jersey, Nevada, and New York. A couple of states clearly don't fit the trend: Texas and Oklahoma have relative large increases in nonwhite population but are also states in which Democrats have lost ground over the forty years studied here. Also notable here (and in all three other plots in Figure 4.2) is that there is very little differentiation in political support at relatively low levels of population change. For instance, among those states with the smallest growth in the nonwhite population (less than 2.5 percentage points) are Kentucky and West Virginia, both places with steep declines in Democratic support; South Carolina, where party support barely changes; and Maine, New Hampshire, and Vermont, all states where Democrats made impressive gains. This is similar to the patterns found for the effects of foreign-born population and, to a lesser extent,

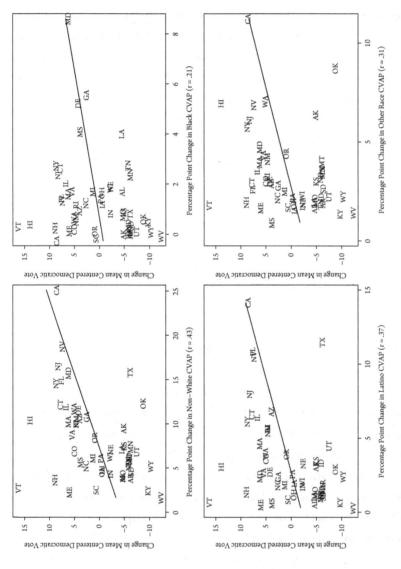

Figure 4.2 Changes in Racial and Ethnic Composition of States and Changes in Party Support in Presidential Elections, 1972–80 to 2004–12

NOTE: The dependent variable in all scatter plots is change in estimated Democratic support from 1972–80 to 2004–12, based on the trend in the Democratic share of the two-party vote, centered around the national two-party division (see Figures 1.3 and 1.4). The independent variables are measured as the change in their average value from 1972–80 to 2004–12.

weighted internal migration (Figure 3.2). As in the case of foreign-born migrations, this pattern probably indicates that changes in population need to be nontrivial before they register a systematic impact on changes in political support.

Decomposing the change in nonwhite population reveals a few differences across subgroups. Looking first at changes in the size of the black population (upper right quadrant), there simply isn't much of a connection to changes in party support. One potential explanation for this is that most states did not see substantial changes in the size of their black population. Interestingly four states actually saw slight decreases in blacks as a percentage of CVAP (California, Idaho, South Carolina, and West Virginia), and in one state (Alaska) there was no change. Overall forty states had increases in the black CVAP of 2 or fewer percentage points. Among the states with the greatest increases there is a slight tendency toward improved Democratic position, but the trend is not strong enough to constitute much of a relationship (r =.21, p =.14). The pattern for change in Latino CVAP is strikingly similar to that for change in nonwhite population overall, reflecting the fact that the greatest source of change in nonwhite population is linked to the growth in the Latino population. The range of change in Latino population is much greater than that for the black population, from less than a single percentage point for several states to just over 14 points for California. The familiar pattern of low differentiation in political change at low levels of population change, coupled with generally high levels of increased Democratic support among the states with the greatest increase in the Latino population, persists. Overall there is a moderate correlation between change in Latino population and change in Democratic votes (r = .37). The same pattern also emerges when considering changes in other nonwhite populations (lower right quadrant), once again led by California, with an increase of just over 11 points, and an overall correlation with changes in Democratic votes of .31. A couple of states stand out across these figures as being somewhat impermeable to the political effects of changes in nonwhite population: Texas, Oklahoma, and, to a lesser extent, Alaska are states that experienced relatively substantial increases in their nonwhite populations (Texas via increased Latino population; Oklahoma and Alaska via increased "other" populations) but grew increasingly Republican over this forty-year time span. So much for any Democratic hope that Texas will turn "blue" due to increases in its Latino population.

All told, changes in racial and ethnic composition have some impact on changes in state support for presidential candidates, but this impact is somewhat limited, at least in this simple bivariate analysis. In particular the effects of changing composition seem to be felt primarily in those states where truly substantial changes have taken place. With the exception of a couple of already noted cases, states with above-average increases in the nonwhite population also had increases in Democratic vote share from the early 1970s to the 2010s. Political change was much more heterogeneous among states with below-average increases in the nonwhite population, indicating that political change in some of those states must be explained by some other process.

Socioeconomic and Occupational Status

Other demographic characteristics with important links to voting behavior are socioeconomic and occupational status. Four different indicators are used to measure these concepts at the state level: change in the percentage of CVAP whose income falls below the poverty rate, change in the percentage of the workforce who are unionized,[10] change in the percentage of the CVAP workforce who are employed as professionals, and percentage of the CVAP with college education beyond a standard four-year degree. Figure 4.3 presents the bivariate relationships between each indicator of socioeconomic and occupational status and changes in party support for presidential candidates. Here we see a lot of variation in the strength of relationships. For both changes in poverty rate and changes in unionization rates (upper left and upper right panels) there are slightly positive relationships that are barely significant using a one-tailed test (p =.04 and p =.09, respectively).[11] States with below-average changes in poverty moved very slightly Republican (–.87 change in centered Democratic vote), while states with above-average changes in poverty moved 1.7 points in the Democratic direction, on average. The relationship for change in union coverage is of roughly the same magnitude: Democrats lost 1.1 points in centered Democratic vote among states with greater than average declines in union coverage and gained 1.9 points among states with smaller than average union losses. Note, though, that these average gains and losses reflect central tendencies, and there is a lot of variation in outcomes.

The relationships for both occupational status and educational attainment are appreciably stronger. There is a moderately strong positive relationship (r =.46) between change in the percentage of the CVAP workforce with professional occupations and change in centered Democratic vote: Democrats gained 3.7 points in states with above-average increases in professionals, and on average lost 2.01 points in states with below-average growth in professionals. This difference in average outcome (5.7 points) is substantial, especially compared to the differences found for poverty and unionization, and is also larger than that found for change in nonwhite population in Figure 4.2. The pattern is even stronger (r =.65) for the relationship between change in percentage of CVAP with education beyond a four-year college degree and change in centered Democratic vote (lower right quadrant): Democrats gained an average of 5.8 points in states with above-average growth in advanced degrees and lost an average of 2.4 points in states with below-average growth in advanced degrees, for an overall difference between the two groups of 8.2 points. The relationship between education and political outcomes is stronger than that for professional occupations, but the two variables overlap appreciably. This overlap is revealed somewhat by a close inspection of the scatter plots in Figure 4.3, where states with the greatest growth in both professionals and higher education tend to be in the Northeast and Mid-Atlantic region, and states with low levels of both tend to be in the Plains and the South. The connection is further confirmed by a strong positive correlation between the two variables (r =.72).

The results in Figure 4.3 are a bit of a mixed bag. On one hand, changes in poverty and unionization are just barely related to changes in party

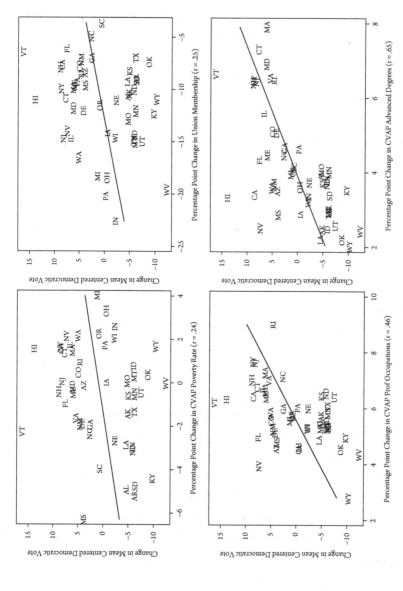

Figure 4.3 Changes in Socioeconomic and Occupational Status in the States and Changes in Party Support in Presidential Elections, 1972–80 to 2004–12

NOTE: The dependent variable in all scatter plots is change in estimated Democratic support from 1972–80 to 2004–12, based on the trend in the Democratic share of the two-party vote, centered around the national two-party division (see Figures 1.3 and 1.4). The independent variables are measured as the change in their average value from 1972–80 to 2004–12.

performance. Although this is a bit at odds with expectations, it bears remembering that the individual-level evidence presented in Figure 4.1 shows that related measures (family income and union household) were not strongly related to vote choice in 2012, and there is increasing evidence of income-related measures taking on less meaning for vote choice as both low- and high-income voters feel cross-pressured by party positions on cultural issues (Ortiz and Stonecash 2009). On the other hand, there are clear patterns in the data supporting the connection between professional occupational status, educational attainment, and presidential votes. As expected, Democrats gained the most ground in states with the greatest increases in professionals and the highly educated and lost the most ground in states with the lowest growth in these groups. This finding is perfectly in keeping with the idea that professionals and the highly educated are increasingly driven to the Democratic Party because of their generally liberal views on social and postmaterial issues (Coan and Holman 2008; Feldman and Johnston 2014; Judis and Teixeira 2004; Ortiz and Stonecash 2009).

Cultural Indicators

Cultural variables increasingly matter to voting behavior and election outcomes (Abramowitz and Saunders 2008; Judis and Teixeira 2004; Leege et al. 2002; Pieper 2011). There is no single state-level indicator that measures cultural liberalism or conservatism of the states, but it is possible to observe changes in demographic characteristics that are typically connected to different sides of the cultural divide. For instance, part of the explanation given for the gender gap and the marriage gap is that men and women differ in important ways on cultural issues (Kaufmann 2002, 2009), as do married and unmarried people (Gerskoff 2009), the expectation being that women and single people are more culturally liberal than men and married people. Perhaps the most obvious cultural fault lines are found in religious differences, primarily differences in religiosity (Olson and Green 2006). The data in Figure 4.4 provide a simple, bivariate look at how changes in variables connected to cultural issues are related to changes in party support in presidential elections. The top two scatter plots focus on changes in the percentage of CVAP who are female (top left) and who are single and never married (top right). The two scatter plots on the bottom use estimates of the percentage of the state population who attend weekly religious services and the number of religious congregations per 10,000 state residents.[12] Despite relatively strong individual-level evidence of substantively important relationships for these variables, there is very little suggestion of significant relationships in Figure 4.4. The slope for change in female percentage of CVAP is nearly flat and the correlation is barely greater than zero. In this particular case part of the explanation for the weak relationship could be that there is not much real change in percentage of female CVAP among the states. With the exception of Alaska and Hawaii, almost all states changed by less than 2 percentage points. Recall from earlier scatter plots that there tends not to be much differentiation on the dependent variable when substantial numbers of states are clustered as low levels of change. This is clearly the case with sex breakdowns but probably does not explain the lack of relationship between change in percentage of single CVAP and change in election outcomes (upper right quadrant), since there is much greater variation in the independent variable. Although there is a slight positive trend to the data on marital status, the correlation is quite small and not statistically significant ($r = .16$, $p = .14$). Interestingly there also is no real evidence of important effects from the measures of religious saturation. In the plot for change in congregations (lower left quadrant) there is a negative trend to the data (seemingly driven by Utah's movement), but again the correlation is small and not significant ($r = -.20$, $p = .14$). The pattern is even weaker for the relationship between change in weekly attenders and change in election outcomes ($r = -.06$, $p = .33$). Simply put, there is no evidence here that *changes* in any of these variables are connected to changes in party support. Note, though, that this is different from saying that states with relatively high levels of religious commitment are not different from states with low levels of commitment, or that states with a high percentage of single people are the same politically as states with a low percentage of single people. It is just saying

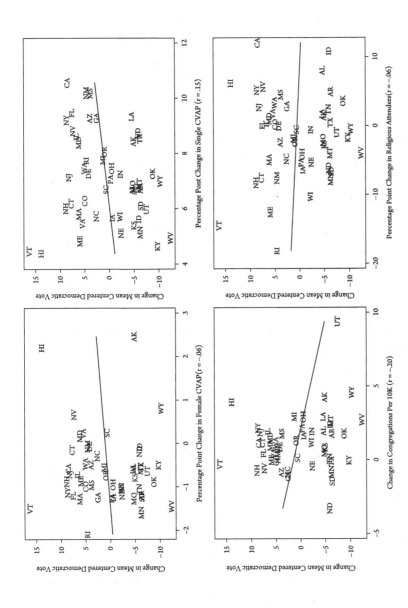

Figure 4.4 Changes in Cultural Indicators in the States and Changes in Party Support in Presidential Elections, 1972–80 to 2004–12

NOTE: The dependent variable in all scatter plots is change in estimated Democratic support from 1972–80 to 2004–12, based on the trend in the Democratic share of the two-party vote, centered around the national two-party division (see Figures 1.3 and 1.4). The independent variables are measured as the change in their average value from 1972–80 to 2004–12.

that changes in these indicators over this period of time are not related to changes in party support. As will become clear in the next chapter, differences in the *levels* of some of these indicators at a given point in time are related to state differences in presidential election outcomes.[13]

COMBINED EFFECTS OF DEMOGRAPHIC CHARACTERISTICS

As interesting as these snapshots of the bivariate relationships are, they don't put us in a position to be as definitive as we could be about the unique effects of each variable. To do this we need to evaluate these variables—or at least a subset of them—in the context of a multivariate model that takes into account the extent to which the characteristics have overlapping relationships to the dependent variable. The goal of this model is to develop a parsimonious set of variables that represent each of the three sets of influences but that also avoids excessive interitem correlation that could lead to high levels of collinearity.[14] For instance, change in the percentage of nonwhite CVAP is selected from the set of race and ethnicity variables rather than specifying change in each of the component groups. In the socioeconomic and occupational status variable, change in poverty, change in unions, and change in percentage with advanced degree are utilized. Change in professionals is not used because it is strongly related to change in advanced degrees (r =.72), is never significant when entered in the same model as advanced degrees (whereas advanced degrees usually is significant), and in some models the correlation with advanced degrees leads to the conclusion that neither change in professional nor change in advanced degrees matters. From the cultural variables, change in congregations per 10,000 population was selected for the model, primarily because it is the most direct measure of one of the most important influences on cultural politics (religious influence),[15] and it is less collinear with noncultural variables than change in percent female, change in percent single, or change in regular attenders.

The first step in the multivariate analysis is to look at the pared down set of five demographic characteristics together and then add dynamic versions of the two measures of migration—change in percent foreign-born and change in the weighted measure of internal migration—used in chapter 3. Table 4.1 presents the set of five demographic indicators in Model 1. Here we see results similar to those found in the separate bivariate scatter plots: both change in nonwhite population and the percentage with advanced degrees are significantly related to change in state-level presidential outcomes, but none of the other variables has a statistically significant effect on changes in votes, either individually or when tested together. The effect of race and ethnicity and education are positive, as anticipated, and the impact of changes in education is particularly pronounced. The second column in Model 1 presents an intuitively clear means of comparing the effects of the independent

Table 4.1 COMPOSITIONAL CHANGE AND CHANGES IN CENTERED DEMOCRATIC VOTE IN PRESIDENTIAL ELECTIONS, 1972–2012

	Change in Centered Democratic Vote					
	Model 1		Model 2		Model 3	
	b/s.e.	$\Delta Y, S_x$	b/s.e.	$\Delta Y, S_x$	b/s.e.	$\Delta Y, S_x$
Δ % Foreign-Born	—		.853	2.33	*.718*	1.97
			.633		.258	
Δ Internal Migration Index	—		**4.809**	1.39	**4.88**	1.41
			2.612		2.625	
Δ % Non-White	**.315**	1.5	−.097	−.47	—	—
	.165		.373			
Δ % Advanced Degree	**2.407**	3.6	**2.16**	3.22	**2.14**	3.18
	.554		.446		.436	
Δ % Union	.341	1.4	.241	.99	.229	.94
	.222		.207		.199	
Δ % Poverty	.603	1.4	.500	1.18	.450	1.06
	.435		.518		.427	
Δ Congregations per 10,000	−.071	−.1	−.012	−.02	−.006	−.01
	.387		.341		.345	

(continued)

Table 4.1 CONTINUED

	Change in Centered Democratic Vote					
	Model 1		Model 2		Model 3	
	b/s.e.	ΔY,S$_x$	b/s.e.	ΔY,S$_x$	b/s.e.	ΔY,S$_x$
Constant	7.64	—	-7.68	—	**-8.27**	—
	4.076		4.327		3.686	
N	50		50		50	
R²	0.559		.619		.618	
Adj. R²	0.509		.555		.564	
Root MSE	4.66		4.43		4.39	

NOTE: All models estimated with robust standard errors. **Bold** = $p < .05$; ***bold italics*** = $p < .01$ (one-tailed); b/s.e. = slope/standard error; and ΔY,S$_x$ = change in the dependent variable for a standard deviation change in the independent variable. The dependent variable is change in estimated Democratic support from 1972–80 to 2004–12, based on the trend in the Democratic share of the two-party vote, centered around the national two-party division (see Figures 1.3 and 1.4).

variables: each coefficient in this column is the amount of change in the centered Democratic vote for a 1 standard deviation change in each of the independent variables. This measure puts the independent variables on equal footing in terms of central tendency and variance and permits a more intuitively clear estimation of relative effect than do the raw coefficients. By the standardized measure, change in advanced degrees has more than twice the impact as change in the nonwhite population: a standard deviation change in nonwhite population produces a change in centered Democratic vote of 1.5 points, while a standard deviation change in percentage with advanced degree leads to a change in vote of 3.6 points.[16] These findings fit fairly well with expectations related to the changing racial and ethnic composition of state electorates (Judis and Teixeira 2004), as well as those related to the changing size of the well-educated professional class (Hood and McKee 2010; Judis and Teixeira 2004; Manza and Brooks 1999), the primary difference being that education is singled out here as the indicator of the sort of values that may produce more socially liberal preferences of the professional class (Feldman and Johnston 2014).

ADDING MIGRATION TO THE MIX

The story so far fits with the factors that researchers have suspected were moving states toward and away from the Democratic Party: states that grew relatively more nonwhite than other states shifted somewhat toward the Democratic Party, and states with slower growth in the nonwhite population shifted toward the Republican Party;[17] states that saw larger than average increases in the percentage of population with advanced degrees grew substantially more Democratic, while states with smaller than average increases in advanced degrees generally grew more Republican. These effects are impressive, but they may be masking the effects of other variables, in particular variables related to population migration. Importantly both foreign-born and internal migration are tied to changes in party support (see chapter 3) and are also related to changes in race, ethnicity, and levels of education. For instance, the correlation between change in the nonwhite population and change in the foreign-born population in the states is .86, and the correlation between change in percentage with advanced degrees and change in the weighted measure of internal migration is .49. So some of the effects picked up in Model 1 may be attributed to the process that helped produce changes in race, ethnicity, and education, and at the same time, the migration processes may have some independent effects of their own.

The exploration of the relationship between migration and changes in political support presented in chapter 3 focused on how much political change there was in states with relatively low and high levels of foreign-born migrants and liberal internal migrants. The idea was that states with higher levels of population born outside the United States or in other states would have experienced more political change as a result of migration. And indeed the analysis in chapter 3 shows that there are substantively important relationships between the measures of migration and electoral change. However, that analysis examined the relationship between *levels* of migration and political change, not *changes* in levels of migration and political changes. The point of this chapter is to examine changes in population characteristics, including changes in levels of migration. There was some existing level of foreign-born and internal migrant population in the states in the 1970s and 1980s that is highly correlated with levels in the 2000s, and to be confident that changes in migration influence changes in election outcomes we need to measure the level of migration in the 2000s relative to the levels forty years ago. The "change" operationalization is consistent with the measurement of other variables examined so far in this chapter and should increase the level of confidence we can have that the results for migration represent a dynamic process. This is easy enough for the foreign-born population, by simply subtracting the average percentage of foreign-born in 1972–80 from the average in 2004–12. It is a bit more difficult to measure change in the index of internal migrants weighted by the ideology of migrants' birth states, since that index uses a lagged measure of state ideology that is not available prior to the mid-1970s. Still it is possible to calculate what the weighted internal migrant measure would have been in the late 2000s *if migration patterns had not changed* since the earlier time period. To do this Equation 3.1 is recalculated using the internal migration patterns that existed in 1980 rather than in 2008, and the difference between the two can be used as a measure of the change in the political direction of internal migration. (Positive values indicate a more liberal internal migration pattern in the later period.)

Model 2 combines the demographic and migration variables, producing some interesting changes. The most apparent among these is that when entered in the same model, change in percent nonwhite and change in the foreign-born population lose statistical significance. As pointed out earlier, these two variables overlap a lot, and including them in the same model introduces substantial collinearity.[18] Given that the substantive impact of the foreign-born coefficient is barely changed from a model that includes just the migration variables,[19] while the slope for nonwhite population is reduced to virtually zero (in fact is slightly negative), it appears that the effect of nonwhite population is swamped by adding change in foreign-born population to the model. This does not mean that change in the racial and ethnic makeup of the states has no bearing on change in political outcomes, as part of the impact of changes in the foreign-born population stems from the fact that foreign-born migration is a major source of change in racial and ethnic composition. Despite its sustained substantive effect in Model 2, the coefficient for change in foreign-born population loses significance if change in nonwhite population is left in the model. When change in percent nonwhite is dropped from the model (Model 3), the slope for foreign-born population regains significance, and the model fit is relatively unaffected.[20] It is important to understand that this diminution of the effects of change in nonwhite population is not in response to some coincidental overlap between two variables; it is in response to specifying one of the important processes that leads to changes in the racial composition of the electorate: changes in foreign-born migration patterns.

In addition to change in foreign-born population, change in the internal migrant population and change in percentage with advanced degrees also have significant influences on changes in Democratic support in Model 3. Among these variables, change in advanced degrees has the greatest impact, followed by change in foreign-born, and then by change in internal migrants. For changes in advanced degrees and changes in percentage of foreign-born these are fairly stable effects, but the standardized effect of change in weighted internal migration drops off a lot when the other demographic variables are added (see note 19), probably due in part to its relationship to change in advanced degrees ($r = .49$).

PARTY AND IDEOLOGY

To this point my analysis has focused primarily on changes in population demographic characteristics, mostly those that are easily defined and measured by objective methods. However, as discussed in chapter 2, it is important to take into account changes in political tastes at the state level, changes that can be linked to changes in voting behavior. In particular it is important to measure changes in state-level ideology and party identification. Certainly it must be the case that one of the reasons states drift toward supporting Democratic or Republican presidential candidates is that they have experienced changes in the underlying distribution of ideological or partisan preferences, especially given the importance of party and ideology as structuring factors in existing research on presidential outcomes in the states (Holbrook 1991; Rabinowitz et al. 1984; Rosenstone 1983). One of the difficulties in analyzing changes in party and ideology, especially as those changes relate to changes in election outcomes, lies in finding appropriate measures that are empirically distinct from the thing we want to explain: election outcomes. Most contemporary measures of state ideology, for instance, incorporate election outcomes into the measurement itself, either by measuring the ideological tendencies of elected officials from the states (Berry et al. 1998, 2010; Holbrook and Poe 1987) or, for both party and ideology, by using the election results or state demographic characteristics, along with public opinion data, to generate state-level estimates (Enns and Koch 2013; Pacheco 2011). For instance, the measure of state ideology used in chapter 3 to estimate the ideological tendencies of home states for internal migrants is based on hundreds of thousands of survey responses gathered across the fifty states but utilizes presidential election results and state demographic measures as part of a poststratification strategy to help provide more accurate estimates of state ideology (Enns and Koch 2013). This makes it an ideal measure of ideology for the analysis in chapter 3, where I was primarily interested in capturing the political context of the birth states for internal migrants at a given point in time. However, when explaining change in elections over time it is unwise to use a measure that incorporates election outcomes, since at least part of the dependent variable will be embedded in the independent variable. Likewise, because the Enns and Koch (2010) and Pacheco (2011) measures of party and ideology rely on state demographic characteristics in the estimation process, they are not ideal for models that include demographic characteristics, such as the one tested in this chapter.

The best alternative for this analysis is to utilize responses to party identification and ideology questions from national public opinion surveys, aggregated at the state level. This method has been used by others (Carsey and Harden 2010; Wright et al. 1985), but none of the existing measures covers the time period studied here. The data I use are based on the raw—unadjusted—survey data from Enns and Koch's (2013) project on state-level public opinion, which used hundreds of surveys and hundreds of thousands of responses to create poststratified measures of party and ideology.[21] For each state in each election cycle I created a net Democratic Party identification (% Democratic identifiers minus % Republican identifiers) and a net liberal identification (% liberal identifiers minus % conservative identifiers) measure based on the raw state-by-state survey marginal percentages. There are some discontinuities in the data, and many steps were used to create these measures, all of which are summarized in the appendix.

Figure 4.5 presents the bivariate relationships between changes in state-level party identification and ideology and changes in presidential voting. The top panel shows the influence of changes in party identification on changes in votes. There are a couple things to note here. First, focusing just on the horizontal axis, Democrats lost ground in party identification in the overwhelming majority of states, gaining strength in only eight states. This reflects a longer-term secular decline that began in the mid-1960s and gained momentum in the 1980s (Meffert et al. 2001; Petrocik 1987). Second, Democrats generally made their greatest electoral gains in states in which net Democratic identification increased or decreased relatively little, and they suffered their greatest losses in states in which net identification declined substantially. With the exception of Iowa, the other seven states where Democrats increased their identification advantage (Connecticut, Delaware, Hawaii, Illinois, New Hampshire, New York, and Vermont) are all states where Democrats made significant gains. Further, on average, Democrats gained 2.6 points in states with above-average change in Democratic identification and lost 1.8 points in states with below-average change in Democratic identification. This pattern is further reflected in the correlation coefficient (.44), which indicates a moderate positive relationship. The impact of changes in ideology on changes in votes is presented in the bottom

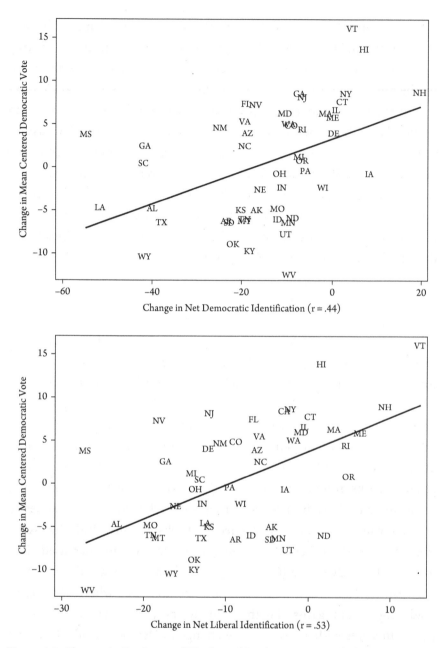

Figure 4.5 Changes in Partisan and Ideological Predispositions and Changes in Party Support in Presidential Elections, 1972–76 to 2004–12

NOTE: The dependent variable is change in estimated Democratic support from 1972–80 to 2004–12, based on the trend in the Democratic share of the two-party vote, centered around the national two-party division (see Figures 1.3 and 1.4). The independent variables are measured as the change in their average value from 1972–80 to 2004–12.

scatter plot in Figure 4.5. Akin to party identification, net liberal identification declined over time in most states, increasing in just nine states,[22] and the scatter plot and correlation (r = .53) show a moderate positive relationship between change in ideology and change in votes. On average, Democrats gained 3.5 points in states with above-average change in liberal identification and lost two points in states with below-average change in liberal identification.

The final part of the analysis focuses on the combined effects of party, ideology, and demographic characteristics on presidential outcomes, as well as the extent to which changes in demographic characteristics influence changes in party and ideology. The first two models in Table 4.2 provide a test of the impact of party and ideology together, as well as in a model alongside demographic change variables. When considered together, impact of changes in party identification is diminished and not statistically significant, while ideology maintains both substantive and statistical significance.[23] However, when demographic

Table 4.2 CHANGES IN STATE POLITICAL PREDISPOSITIONS AND CHANGES IN CENTERED DEMOCRATIC VOTE

	Change in Centered Democratic Vote		Change in Ideology	Change in Party Identification
	Model 1	Model 2	Model 3	Model 4
	b/s.e.	b/s.e.	b/s.e.	b/s.e.
Δ Liberal Advantage	**0.318**	0.101		
	0.122	0.108		
Δ Democratic Advantage	0.068	0.039		
	0.069	0.074		
Δ % Foreign-Born		*0.793*	−0.574	−0.456
		0.245	0.402	0.711
Δ Weighted Internal Migration		3.947	6.152	8.009
		2.529	3.831	7.189
Δ % Advanced Degree		*1.798*	*1.953*	*3.694*
		0.495	0.624	1.085

(continued)

Table 4.2 CONTINUED

	Change in Centered Democratic Vote		Change in Ideology	Change in Party Identification
	Model 1	Model 2	Model 3	Model 4
	b/s.e.	b/s.e.	b/s.e.	b/s.e.
Δ % Union		0.168	*0.889*	−0.725
		0.211	0.295	0.479
Δ % Poverty		0.21	**1.379**	*2.571*
		0.431	0.552	0.899
Δ Congregations per 10,000		−0.012	0.308	−0.631
		0.409	0.858	1.209
Constant	*4.182*	−6.184	−6.136	*−37.088*
	1.146	4.416	5.168	9.605
N	50	50	50	50
R²	0.295	0.641	0.443	0.493
Adjusted R²	0.265	0.570	0.366	0.422
RMSE	5.695	4.354	7.124	11.656

NOTE: All models estimated with robust standard errors. **Bold** = $p < .05$; ***bold italics*** = $p < .01$ (one-tailed); and b/s.e. = slope/ standard error. The dependent variable in Models 1 and 2 is change in estimated Democratic support from 1972–80 to 2004–12, based on the trend in the Democratic share of the two-party vote, centered around the national two-party division (see Figures 1.3 and 1.4); the dependent variable in Model 3 is change in the average net liberal identification from 1972–80 to 2004–12; the dependent variable in Model 4 is change in the average net Democratic identification from 1972–80 to 2004–12.

variables are added to the model, both party and ideology are reduced to trivial influences. This is because their explanation of vote change overlaps with the statistical explanation provided by the set of demographic characteristics. Models 3 and 4 in Table 4.2 provide a sense of how much of the observed change in party and ideology is attributable to changes in demographic characteristics. In the case of political ideology, as a group, changes in demographic variables account for about

37% of variance in changes from the 1970s to the 2010s, and changes in advanced degrees, poverty rate, and union membership stand out as particularly important, with change in poverty rate also making a significant contribution. In the case of changes in party identification (Model 4), demographic characteristics explain slightly more variation than for ideology, and changes in advanced degrees and poverty are also important influences.[24] These results are important in illustrating that part of the mechanism by which changes in demographic characteristics lead to changes in election outcomes is by altering the underlying political predilections of the states.

CHANGING POPULATIONS AND CHANGING ELECTION OUTCOMES

A frequently offered explanation for changes in state-level voting patterns points to growth in certain population groups—usually racial minorities and well-educated professionals—as well as changes in the geographic distribution of those groups. Put very simply, the proposition is that states have become more Democratic or Republican over time in response to changes in their population characteristics. This idea has been subjected to empirical scrutiny here and largely finds a lot of support. But all population changes are not of equal consequence. The evidence I presented points to three important sources of political change in the states: changes in the percentage of the state CVAP who are foreign-born, changes in the pattern of internal migration among the CVAP, and changes in the percentage of state CVAP who are educated beyond a four-year college degree. States with significant gains in foreign-born population increased their support for Democratic presidential candidate, while states with declines in or low levels of foreign-born growth tended to move toward Republican presidential candidates. States whose patterns of internal migration shifted toward more liberal source states grew more Democratic, while states that shifted to more conservative source states moved toward Republican candidates. And states with relatively large

increases in the share of the population with more than a four-year college degree became markedly more supportive of Democratic presidential
candidates, while those with slower growth in the highly educated population became more supportive of Republican candidates. The impact of
changes in advanced degrees cannot be overstated: in every instance—
whether explaining changes in votes or changes in party and ideology—
changes in the percent with advanced education have had an important
effect on all outcomes.

I have not discussed two hypothetically important sources of political change—changes in race and ethnicity and changes in the professional occupation class—as having substantial empirical effects. This is
not because these variables are unimportant but because their effects are
largely subsumed by two other variables: change in foreign-born population (strongly correlated with change in nonwhite population) and change
in advanced degrees (strongly correlated with change in professional population). Changes in racial composition and professional occupations are
related to changes in presidential votes. In fact when Model 3 of Table 4.1 is
reestimated with change in nonwhite population substituted for change in
foreign-born and change in percentage of professionals is substituted for
change in percentage with advanced degrees, both variables are significant
and show that Democratic fortunes have grown in states with the largest
increases in percent nonwhite and percent professional and decline in states
with the slowest growth in nonwhite and professional population (analysis not shown). However, substituting these variables comes at substantial
cost in explanatory power, with the adjusted R^2 dropping from .56 to .44.
So it is not that changes in race, ethnicity, and professional occupations
don't matter to changes in state-level presidential election outcomes—they
do—but that their effects are captured as part of the effects of changes in
foreign-born and highly educated shares of the population.

Figure 4.6 provides a sense of how well the model tested here explains
actual changes in presidential election outcomes in the states. The vertical
axis is the *actual* change in centered Democratic share of the two-party
vote in the states from 1972–80 to 2004–12, and the horizontal axis is the
predicted change, based on the regression results presented in Model 2 of

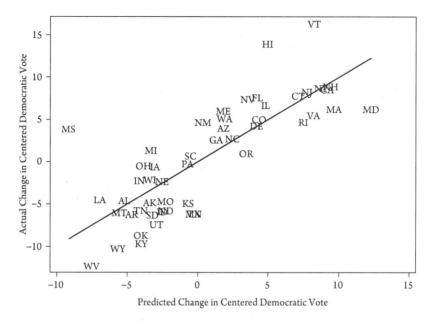

Figure 4.6 Predicted and Actual Changes in Centered Democratic Vote Share, 1972–80 to 2004–12

NOTE: The dependent variable is change in estimated Democratic support from 1972–80 to 2004–12, based on the trend in the Democratic share of the two-party vote, centered around the national two-party division (see Figures 1.3 and 1.4). The independent variable is the predicted change in estimate Democratic vote based on the regression slopes from Model 2 of Table 4.2, multiplied times the values of all of the corresponding independent variables.

Table 4.2. The predicted changes are calculated based on state outcomes on each of the independent variables and the slopes for those independent variables. Generally speaking, the actual outcomes track pretty closely with the predicted outcomes: states with changes in characteristics that are associated with increased Democratic support generally moved in the Democratic direction, and states whose populations changed in ways that augur for increased Republican support generally moved in that direction. There are a few states that are substantially more off diagonal than other states: Hawaii, Vermont, and especially Mississippi all became more Democratic than expected, given their population changes during this time period. It is usually best not to become too preoccupied with explaining specific data points. Still it is worth pointing out that part of Hawaii's deviance is probably due to a "favorite son" effect for President Obama, who was born in Hawaii, since the home-state variable used when estimating the trend in Democratic support only controlled for the state from which the candidates were running. Mississippi is a bit of a mystery, since none of its outcomes on the independent variables would point to any reason it should move toward the Democratic Party. At the same time, Mississippi's increase of 4 points in Democratic support should not be confused with Democratic candidates having any chance of winning there or with Mississippi being a Democratic state. From 2004 to 2012 Democratic candidates ran 8.6 points below their national vote share in Mississippi, and only sixteen states have been less supportive of Democratic candidates. In short, Democrats have improved their lot in Mississippi a bit but still stand very little chance of winning.

It is also interesting to note that certain variables did not show up to the dance. For instance, in both the bivariate and multivariate models there is no sign of anything resembling a relationship between change per capita in religious congregations and change in presidential voting patterns. Similarly, although changes in party identification and ideology are related to changes in votes in the bivariate analysis, their effect is minimal in the multivariate analysis. In the case of party and ideology, part of the explanation for minimal effects is found in the overlap both variables have with the other independent variables. For change in religious congregations, however, the explanation might be that there simply wasn't very much meaningful change. To be sure all states changed somewhat, but states that were very religious by this metric in the 1970s were also very religious in the 2010s. While there has been absolute change in religious saturation in the states, there hasn't been a lot of relative change. In fact the correlation between religious congregations per 10,000 residents in the 1970s and in the 2010s is .93. Given the limited change in relative religiosity, it is perhaps not surprising that *change* in religiosity is not related to *change* in votes.

Chapter 5 takes a different perspective on explaining change in party support, looking not at changes in the values of independent variables but at changes in the relationships between independent and dependent variables. So, for instance, state religiosity (measured with congregations per capita) might not have an impact on changes in votes when measured as a change variable, but its effect on election outcomes in any given election cycle may have changed over time in such a way that election outcomes are different now than they would have been if the relationship had not changed. The same may be true for other variables in the analysis. It may well be that some variables that were not connected to change in votes in this chapter still play a role in shaping changes in party support as a consequence of how their relationship to votes has changed over time.

Changing Political Context and Changing State Outcomes

The argument explored in chapter 4 was fairly straightforward: certain types of groups are more likely to support Democratic candidates, while others are more likely to support Republican candidates, and as the balance of group strength in the state electorate shifts over time, so too will support for presidential candidates, in accord with the partisan connections of those groups. In short, party support in presidential elections responds to compositional changes in the state electorate. In this chapter the focus shifts to an examination of another way in which group characteristics influence election outcomes: by interacting with the broader political environment to produce different effects on outcomes in different political contexts. I revisit the underlying contextual argument and specify a process that focuses on changes in party elites' behavior, changes in popular perceptions of party elites, and (as a consequence) changes in patterns of group-based determinants of state outcomes. I then provide empirical support for the model and demonstrate important ways in which the effects of demographic and political variables on election outcomes have evolved over time. I use the changes in relationships over time to get a sense of how much these changes have affected outcomes and also to assess the magnitude of these effects compared to the effects of changes in demographic characteristics.

THE CONTEXTUAL MODEL

The argument laid out in chapter 2 and outlined here borrows heavily from work on issue evolution (Carmines and Stimson 1989), partisan sorting (Fiorina et al. 2004; Levendusky 2009), and more generally from work on cue-taking from political elites (Hetherington 2001; Zaller 1991). To reiterate, group connections with political parties are derived from party-based group benefits or from within-group preference homogeneity (broadly, ideology) that align the group with one of the parties. For instance, from the perspective of group benefits, organized labor benefits for the pro-labor polices of the Democratic Party and business interests and wealthy individuals benefit from the pro-business and antitax policies of the Republican Party. In terms of preferences, some groups (nonreligious, unmarried, and highly educated) are likely to hold liberal views on social and cultural issues, while others (religious, married, low level of education) hold conservative and traditional views on social and cultural issues. The argument made in chapter 2 is that these group-based connections to parties are easier to make as interparty ideological differences grow and intraparty differences shrink.

Figure 5.1 spells out the process by which changes in the political climate produce changes in state-level presidential election outcomes. On the right side of the model is a collection of state demographic and political characteristics, which, in any single election cycle, should be related to the election outcomes (represented by the arrow connecting characteristics to outcomes). However, we do not expect that the relationships between these state characteristics and election outcomes are constant over time. Instead they change in response to changes in the national political context, described on the left side of the figure. Here the model assumes that increased party divergence among elites helps clarify how group interests and political preferences align with the parties. Rather than emphasizing single-issue divergence, I focus on ideological polarization between the national parties. However, polarization of elites will not affect voting behavior if it goes mostly unnoticed, so the second step in the process is mass awareness of party differences, which should grow in

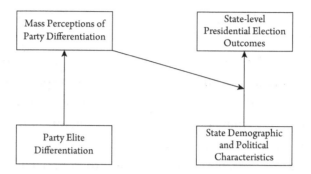

Figure 5.1 Contextual Model of State-Level Presidential Election Outcomes

response to increases in party differentiation among elites. This increased awareness ("clarity," to use Carmines and Stimson's [1989] terminology) then affects the relationship between state characteristics and election outcomes. In effect these changing relationships reflect a "demographic sort" that is facilitated by increased ideological and issue polarization at the elite level (Abramowitz 2010).

The next section illustrates (a) increased polarization of party elites, (b) increased public perception of party differentiation, and (c) increased importance of state demographic and political characteristics as determinants of state-level presidential election outcomes. Demonstrating these factors, however, tells us only that the context and group-based relationships have changed in a way that *could* affect outcomes, not the extent to which outcomes are actually affected. That is the final, and perhaps thorniest, piece of the analysis and will be followed by a comparison to the impact of changing characteristics on outcomes.

CHANGING PARTIES

The first piece of the model is perhaps the easiest to demonstrate, as the polarization of party elites is a well-documented phenomenon (Abramowitz 2010; Fiorina et al. 2004; Hetherington 2001; Levendusky 2009, 2010; McCarty et al. 2006). One of the primary methods for judging ideological divergence is Poole and Rosenthal's (1985) DW-NOMINATE score, which is based on roll call voting behavior of members of Congress. Using information on roll call voting in both the U.S. House of Representatives and the Senate, Poole and Rosenthal are able to estimate the ideological position of members of Congress on a standard liberal-conservative dimension. Aggregating these scores by party over time allows us to get a sense of the extent of change in the polarization of congressional Democrats and Republicans. It is also possible to estimate DW-NOMINATE scores for incumbent presidents based on their public support for and opposition to pieces of legislation.[1] Of course, with presidents it isn't possible to estimate presidential ideology for both parties in a given time period, since only one party at a time holds the White House. Nevertheless it is possible to measure the differences in Democratic and Republican presidential ideology over time.

Figure 5.2 provides estimates of partisan differences in congressional and presidential ideology from 1951 to 2014, spanning the 82nd to 113th Congresses.[2] The top row of plots illustrates the partisan differences on the first dimension of the DW-NOMINATE scores separately for the House (top left) and the Senate (top right). The distance between the Democratic (dark circles) and Republican (gray triangles) lines represents the level of ideological polarization. The patterns in the House show a slight but steady Democratic drift in the liberal direction throughout the time period, while Republicans changed very little until the mid-1970s, at which point they began to grow increasingly conservative at a pronounced rate that accelerated in the early 1990s. Overall Republicans grew more conservative than the Democrats grew liberal. The general trends in the Senate are similar to those in the House, but some of the particulars are a bit different. From the mid-1950s to the mid-1960s there was a pronounced liberal shift in the Democratic Party, followed by a modest trend toward increased liberalism since then. On the Republican side, again, there was little real change until the mid-1970s, when Republicans began to drift in the conservative direction, picking up the pace in the 2000s.

The graph in the lower left corner of Figure 5.2 summarizes information from the top two graphs in terms of the key point of interest: changes in the level of polarization. The lines in this plot represent the

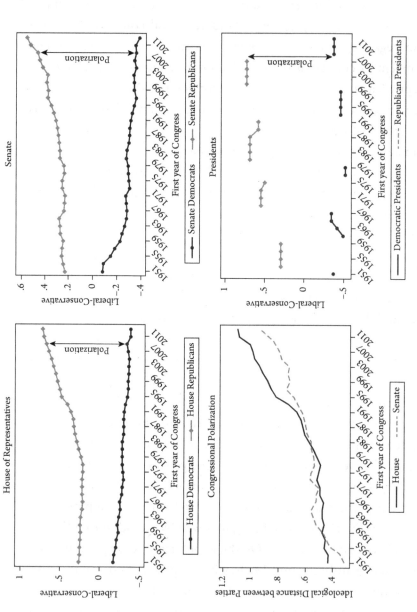

Figure 5.2 Congressional and Presidential Partisan Polarization, 82nd to 113th Congresses

NOTE: All data represent trends in ideological polarization between the parties based on roll call votes in Congress. Standard DW-NOMINATE scores are used for the House and Senate estimates and were obtained from voteview.com. Presidential scores are based on the "common space" DW-NOMINATE scores, vertical distance between the average Democratic and Republican DW-NOMINATE scores for the House (solid line) and the Senate (dashed line). If it wasn't already apparent, this graph makes clear that there has been a sharp increase in polarization in recent decades. Polarization in the House increased very gradually up until the late 1970s, at which point there was a significant upturn in the rate of increase that was maintained through the 2010s. The Senate saw a jump in polarization in the 1950s and 1960s, followed by a fairly stable period until the late 1970s, at which point the pace of increase in polarization quickened significantly. By the 2010s both the House and the Senate were more polarized than at any point in this time period. In fact both are more polarized now than at any point since 1879.[3]

The graph in the lower right quadrant of Figure 5.2 presents data on the ideological positions of Democratic and Republican presidents during the same time period (the last two years of Truman's final term to the first two years of Obama's second term). These data are a bit different on a couple of counts. First, unlike the House and Senate data, only one party holds the White House at a time, so for each presidential term we have data on only one party. Second, the "party" measure for the presidency is based on only one person rather than dozens for the Senate and hundreds for the House. Although the president clearly represents his party, it is possible that the idiosyncrasies of individual presidents could make it difficult to discern trends in the data. This does not appear to be a problem, however, as the pattern for presidents looks somewhat like the pattern for members of Congress. For Democratic presidents there is very little change in presidential ideology over time. In fact the correlation between "year" and DW-NOMINATE scores for Democratic presidents is a paltry .06. For Republican presidents, on the other hand, there is a clear trend toward increasing conservatism over time. Whereas there was no relationship between time and ideology among Democratic presidents, the correlation between year and ideology for Republican presidents is .90. The result of these trends is increased ideological divergence as a function of which party occupies the White House.

The data in Figure 5.2 make very clear an already well-known point about contemporary American politics: political elites from the two major parties have become increasingly polarized at the national level. Whether in the House, the Senate, or the White House, the gap between parties continues to grow over time in a way that not only affects national political institutions but also may have important effects on voting behavior and election outcomes in presidential contests.

PERCEPTIONS OF PARTY DIFFERENCES

The growing chasms between Democratic and Republican political elites summarized in Figure 5.2 are an important piece of the argument regarding increased structure, or predictability, to state-level presidential outcomes. As parties grow more distinct, state-level outcomes should become more responsive to differences in state demographic and political characteristics. However, the intermediary step between political elites and changes in the structure of election outcomes requires that the public is exposed to, and grows increasingly aware of, party differences.[4] If changes in elite behavior go unnoticed by voters—if growing polarization creates no increase in awareness of ideological and other differences between the parties—then election outcomes in the states should be driven by roughly the same factors now as they were forty years ago.

Support for this important intermediary link is offered in Figure 5.3, which shows the trends in three different measures of perceptions of party differences: the solid line represents the average perceived difference between the parties on a 7-point ideology scale (the positive values show that in all cases the Republican Party was viewed as the more conservative party); the dotted line shows the average perceived ideological difference between the two major party presidential candidates, using the same scale; and the dashed line shows the percentage of respondents who report seeing important differences between the Democratic and Republican parties.[5] As anticipated, the general public is pretty good at picking up trends in elite movement. The solid line represents perceptions of ideological differences between the parties and shows a relatively flat trend from 1972 to 1988 and an upward trend beginning in 1992 and continuing through the 2012 election.[6] The trend in perceived ideological

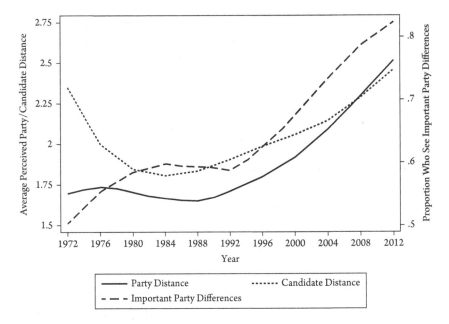

Figure 5.3 Public Perceptions of Candidate and Party Differences, 1972–2012

NOTE: All data are taken from the presidential year ANES surveys. The party and candidate ideological distance lines are based on average responses to questions that asked respondents to rate the parties and candidates on a 7-point scale. Positive values indicate that Republicans are viewed as more conservative than Democrats. The important party difference line is based on the percentage of respondents who said they saw important differences between the two major parties. More details are available in the data appendix. All lines are lowess lines, used to summarize the general trend in the data series.

differences between the presidential candidates (dotted line) looks a bit different, with relatively sharp differences in 1972 and 1976, bottoming out from 1980 to 1988, and again trending upward from 1992 to 2012. The proportion of respondents who report seeing important differences between the parties (dashed line, right vertical axis) increased from 1972 to 1980, was fairly flat from 1980 to 1992, and increased steadily from that point on.

Taken together these trends tell us that Americans' views of parties and candidates underwent a transformation between the early 1970s and the 2010s, a transformation that reflects the trend in polarization of party elites over time. With the exception of stark differences in perceived

candidate ideology in the 1972 Nixon-McGovern contest, generally perceptions of party and candidate ideological differences took an upward
turn sometime around 1992 and continued to increase from that point
on. The relatively high level of candidate differentiation in 1972, while
out of step with the measures of party differences, does serve as a good
indicator of the public's ability to sniff out important differences between
presidential candidates, even if the parties are not as far apart. Perhaps not
surprisingly the source of this gap in candidate placement can be traced
to ratings of Senator George McGovern of South Dakota, whom the public perceived as the most liberal candidate during this time span, rather
than ratings of President Richard Nixon, who was viewed as relatively
moderate among Republican candidates. The perceptions of McGovern,
widely known to represent the liberal, antiwar wing of the Democratic
Party, were on the mark, as his voting record in the Senate makes him
the most liberal Democratic candidate during the period under study
(1972–2012).[7]

The patterns of candidate perceptions presented in Figure 5.3 appear
to track well with changes in party polarization at the elite level; this is
supported by a simple correlational analysis. Specifically the correlations
between averages of House and Senate polarization and public perceptions outlined above are .49 for candidate ideological distance (.75 if 1972
is excluded), .80 for party ideological distance, and .87 for perception of
important party differences. These correlations provide strong support
for the link between elite behavior and public perception of elites outlined
in Figure 5.1.

CHANGING RELATIONSHIPS

This evidence supports two important pieces of the contextual model.
First, party elites have diverged ideologically over the past several decades,
both in Congress and in the White House. This is not new to students of
American politics, but it is an important trend to establish. Second, public
perceptions of party differences follow a pattern expected to flow from

increasingly polarized parties: over time the mass public has come to see greater ideological distance between the parties and, more generally and broadly, to articulate that there are important differences between the parties. The next stage of the analysis is to demonstrate that these changes in elite behavior and public perceptions generally coincide with changes in the mix of state characteristics that shape state-level presidential election outcomes.

Just to be clear, the expectation is that increased ideological polarization of party elites elevates the importance of state-level demographic and political characteristics as determinants of state-level outcomes. There are two ways to evaluate this. First, several characteristics will be evaluated individually to see if their correlation with election outcomes grows stronger over time. Here we are looking at the cross-sectional relationships between state characteristics and state outcomes. But we will be looking at how those relationships change over time, so there is also a dynamic component to this analysis, but not in the same way as the "change" models tested in chapter 4. Another way of thinking about this analysis, or about the way elite polarization might transform presidential elections in the states, is that we are expecting increased structure, or predictability, to state-level outcomes over time. So the second part of this analysis focuses on how well combinations of variables explain state-level outcomes over time, the expectation being that a model of state demographic and political variables should explain greater variance in state outcomes as party elites diverge ideologically.

The first part of this analysis examines the cross-sectional relationships between nine separate variables—net party identification, net ideology, percentage with advanced degrees, percent professional occupations, percent nonwhite, percent foreign-born, union membership, religious congregations for 10,000 population, and percent single—and Democratic share of the two-party vote. In order to avoid potentially confounding effects of other short-term factors, I consider the partial correlation for each of these variables, controlling for presidential and vice-presidential home-state advantage in all years and the southern regional effect during the Carter and Clinton candidacies. Based on earlier discussions, there should be a clear trend toward increasing importance, which will be reflected in increasingly strong partial correlations (positive or negative, depending on the variable and nature of the relationship) between the independent variables and Democratic vote share. If there is no support for the expectation—if voting patterns change little or not at all in response to national context—then we may find relatively constant partial correlations or perhaps a seemingly random pattern, or even (I suppose) increasingly weaker relationships over time.

The first evidence of increased connections between state characteristics and election outcomes is presented in Figure 5.4. Here each of the solid dots represents the partial correlation between the state characteristic and Democratic vote share in a single election year, and the solid line is the trend in the strength of the relationship over time.[8] When interpreting these figures it is important to bear in mind that the vertical axis is not the same for each variable. Because of the range of relationships—some strong, some weak; some positive, some negative—each of the individual plots is rescaled according to the relationship found in the plot. A quick glance at this figure suggests strong support for increased activation of state characteristics as vote predictors over time. In almost every case the partial correlations bounce around a bit in the early part of the series, and then somewhere around 1988 or 1992 the relationships begin to grow in strength, reaching their peak in the 2008 or 2012 elections. It is particularly interesting that for many variables (advanced degrees, professionals, foreign-born, union membership) there was a relatively strong connection to state outcomes in the early part of the series, especially in the 1972 election. While this detracts a bit from the expected trend in relationships, it supports the underlying point that many characteristics can be triggered by the context of the election. In a year when Democrats ran a liberal, antiwar candidate against an incumbent Republican president, many state characteristics assumed prominence as election predictors.

Many interesting patterns emerge here. Looking first at political characteristics, we see that net Democratic Party affiliation was actually negatively related to Democratic votes in the 1972 election and only modestly related from 1976 to 1988 (on average) and grew consistently more

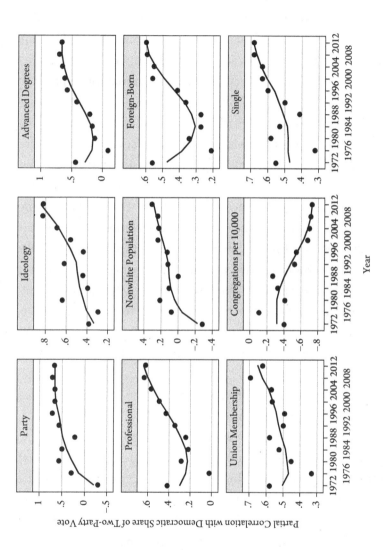

Figure 5.4 Evolving Relationships between State Political and Demographic Characteristics and Democratic Presidential Votes, 1972–2012

NOTE: The black dots represent the partial correlation coefficient for the relationship between each independent variable and the Democratic share of the two-party vote, controlling for presidential and vice-presidential home-state advantage, as well as the southern regional effect during the Carter and Clinton candidacies. The trend line is a lowess line, used to capture the general trend among the individual data points.

important from 1992 to 2012. A somewhat similar pattern emerges with net liberal ideology, although it had a moderate and positive relationship to vote in 1972, a strong relationship in 1980 that receded in 1984, and steadily grew in importance from that point on. One thing that was going on with party and ideology during the 1970s and 1980s was that the process of partisan sorting had not yet run its course, and there were many states that were both Democratic and conservative. This is why net Democratic affiliation was negatively related to Democratic support at the polls in 1972: some of the most Democratic states—southern states— were also some of the most conservative states, and ideology turned out to matter more in the year of the McGovern candidacy. While southern states were ready to abandon liberal Democratic presidential candidates, they continued to support state and local (mostly centrist or conservative) Democratic candidates and had not yet quite sorted themselves into a conservative and Republican bin. In fact the correlation between state ideology and state party affiliation averaged only .08 from 1972 to 1988, grew to .28 for 1996 to 2000, and averaged a much stronger .65 from 2004 to 2012. It appears that just as individuals sorted themselves into the complementary ideological and partisan bins in response to elite polarization, which helped them figure out "what goes with what" (Levendusky 2009, 2010), the states have gone through a similar process of sorting themselves into consistent ideological and partisan groups. As party and ideology increasingly pull in the same direction rather than at cross-purposes, their effects on election outcomes also increased.

Turning to occupational and socioeconomic variables, we see a lot of overlapping patterns. For percent advanced degrees, percent professional, and percent belonging to labor unions, there was a pronounced positive effect in 1972, followed by a precipitous drop-off in 1976, and a steady increase in the impact of these variables from 1980 to 2012. By the 2008 and 2012 elections these variables had average correlations with Democratic votes in excess of .60. Considering percent nonwhite and percent foreign-born, the pattern is similar to those found for other variables, but overall it is much stronger for percent foreign-born. In 1972 there was a negative correlation between nonwhite population and Democratic support, again probably reflecting the conservative South's reaction to the McGovern candidacy (where the percent nonwhite was much higher than in the rest of the country), but the relationship became positive in the 1980s and grew in strength somewhat from 1992 onward. Still, despite the growth in strength, the relationship between nonwhite population and Democratic vote is relatively modest compared to other state characteristics, with a correlation, on average, of .26 from 2004 to 2008. Percent foreign-born, on the other hand, had a particularly pronounced effect in 1972, fell to much weaker effects during from 1976 to 1988, and increased steadily through the 1990s and 2000s. By 2008 and 2012 the partial correlation for percent foreign-born stood at .59.

The two cultural indicators—religious congregations per capita and percent single—also follow a pattern that is consistent with the contextual model. In the case of religious congregations, the effects bounce around a bit and range from weak to moderate (and negative, as expected) during the 1970s and 1980s, increase in strength in 1992 and 1996, and grow even stronger beginning in 2000. Percent single has a somewhat different pattern. The impact of percent single was a bit uneven during the 1970s and 1980s but still averaged a correlation of .48 with Democratic share of the vote. The correlation began a steady increase in 1992, averaging .66 from 2000 to 2012. This pattern dovetails nicely with the increased polarization of elites as well as with other evidence of an increased partisan divide in matters of public opinion.

Although there is a bit of bouncing around in the early set of elections covered in Figure 5.4, there is a very consistent trend toward increasingly strong relationships over time. This trend is generally clear whether one relies on the individual data points or the smoothed trend line. And while this information makes the point very clear, it is also useful to examine one of the variables more closely and focus on what those changing relationships look like across the fifty states and eleven presidential elections. Figure 5.5 presents individual scatter plots for the bivariate relationship between religious congregations per capita and Democratic share of the two-party presidential vote separately for each election from 1972 to 2012.[9] This measure of religious saturation is nicely suited for illustrative purposes in part because it had no discernible relationship to change in election outcomes in the "demographic change" analysis in chapter 4 but emerges as an important variable in Figure 5.4. There is a very clear unfolding of a relationship in Figure 5.5 that provides an important visual representation of what's happening under the hood that produces the changing correlations observed in Figure 5.4. The state abbreviations represent the joint outcomes of Democratic vote share and congregations per capita, and the solid line is the regression line, which summarizes the linear trend in the data. Generally the steeper the regression line and the tighter the states are clustered around the regression line, the stronger the relationship. In the early part of the series we see a fairly modest negative relationship between congregations and election outcomes in 1972, virtually flat regression lines with states fairly widely dispersed in 1976 and 1980, and then a return to modest negative relationships in 1984 and 1988. During this time period presidential outcomes were differentiated somewhat by the concentration of religious congregations, but neither strongly nor consistently. Then, beginning in 1992, the relationship grew increasingly negative, producing steeper regression lines and increased clustering around those lines. By 2012 the simple correlation had grown to .73 (the same as the partial correlation). Particularly notable here is that the predicted outcomes for relatively religious and nonreligious states, on average, do not differ much at all in the early years but are very different in the later years.

How is it that this relationship evolved the way it did? One possible explanation is that the identity of states with relatively high (low) levels of religious saturation changed appreciably over time—in other words, some states grew more religious while others grew less religious—and this created a better alignment between those states and their political preferences. The problem with this explanation, however, is that there was not much *relative* change in state religious saturation over time. As I mentioned in chapter 4, the correlation between religious congregations per 10,000 in the 1970s and 2010s is .93, and a visual inspection of the scatter plots in Figure 5.5 shows that roughly the same states appear over time in the high and low ranges of religious congregations. The more

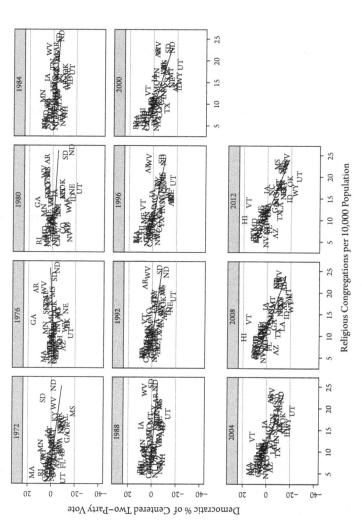

Figure 5.5 The Changing Nature of the Relationship between Religious Congregations per 10,000 Population and Centered Democratic Share of the Two-Party Presidential Vote, 1972–2012

NOTE: Each scatter plot represents the relationship between the number of religious congregations per 10,000 residents and the Democratic share of the state two-party vote, centered on the Democratic share of the national two-party vote. The state abbreviations represent the joint outcomes of religious concentration and Democratic vote share; the solid line in each scatter plot is a regression line that summarizes the linear trend in the data.

likely explanation is the one offered in the discussion of the contextual model: the context of national politics has changed in a way that facilitates bringing into line group interests and preferences with candidate support, and this shapes state outcomes according to the distribution of those groups in the states. This is why we see an increasingly negative regression line as time goes on. Similar to Fiorina et al.'s (2004) notion of polarization at the individual level, it is not the states that have changed, but the substance of politics that connects state populations to the two major parties has changed. This helps explain why changes over time in religion (congregations per 10,000 population), which we recognize today as an important political cleavage, showed no real connection to changes in political outcomes in chapter 4 but emerges as an important influence here.

An important implication of the increases in correlations between state characteristics and state election outcomes is that there is more structure to elections today than there was forty years ago. Put another way, state characteristics should provide a stronger statistical account of state election outcomes today than in the past. Theoretically this is one of the important consequences of the changing political context: as party elites grow more ideologically distinct and group connections to the parties are facilitated, differences in state outcomes should grow more connected to differences in state characteristics. Figure 5.6 provides evidence in support of this idea, displaying the trend in the adjusted R^2 statistic separately for a demographic model, a party and ideology model, and the full model, which includes party, ideology, and demographic characteristics.[10] Here we see that the explanatory power of demographic characteristics declined in strength from 1972 to 1988, rebounded somewhat in 1992, and has increased steadily since then. Party and ideology increase in strength steadily throughout the time period, clearly take a backseat to demographic factors from 1972 to 1984, and then roughly match the strength of demographic characteristics from 1988 to 2012. The full model steadily increases in strength throughout the time period, increasing from an average fit of .56 from 1972 to 1984 to an average fit of .77 from 2000 to 2012. These patterns, along with the others presented

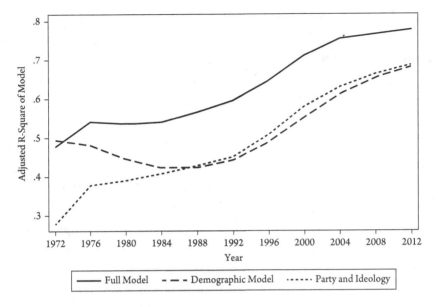

Figure 5.6 Changes in Model Fit, 1972–2012

NOTE: All trend lines are lowess estimates that summarize the trend in the explanatory power of the respective regression models.

in Figures 5.1 to 5.5, jibe quite well with the notion that state characteristics have been activated over time in response to changes in the national political context.

CONDITIONAL EFFECTS

One piece of the model presented in Figure 5.1 that requires a more direct test is the interaction between perceptions of polarization and state demographic characteristics. The arrow from mass perceptions of party differentiation to the arrow connecting demographic characteristics to state-level outcomes reflects the notion that the relationship between demographic characteristics and outcomes is conditioned by perceptions of party differences, which track with actual changes in party polarization. Figures 5.3 through 5.5 provide support for this argument but are not a direct test. In order to get a clearer sense of how individual variables react to changes in party context, I ran a series of separate pooled random-effects regression models in which the seven state characteristics included in the model used in Figure 5.5 interacted with each of the aggregate perception variables (candidate distance, party distance, and important party differences), as well as a measure of congressional polarization. Each model included a state characteristic, one of the conditioning polarization items, the interaction term for the state characteristic and polarization variable, and controls for presidential and vice-presidential home-state advantage, as well as a southern regional control for the Carter and Clinton candidacies. Here I am primarily interested in the direction and significance of the interaction terms, information that is presented in Table 5.1, where there is strong evidence that the relationships between state characteristics and election outcomes are shaped by changes in elite behavior and perceptions of those changes.

A number of important findings emerge in Table 5.1. First, the effects from five of the seven state characteristics (net Democratic identification and percent union being the exceptions) are consistently conditioned by the measures of the national political context. The negative interaction between net Democratic identification and perceived candidate differences is due in part to the low level of party voting in 1972 (see the discussion of the strongly Democratic South earlier in this chapter and Figure 5.4), a year in which perceived candidate difference was at one of its highest values. Second, the strongest conditioning effects are for the measure of actual elite polarization, though the measures of perceptions of polarization do not fall off very much. Third, the strongest effects are found among demographic characteristics rather than party and ideology, supporting the idea that increased elite polarization facilitates the groups-parties connections. Among the demographic characteristics, the slope for religious congregations per 10,000 population stands out as being particularly responsive to the changing political context. I would be remiss, though, if I didn't point out that part of the weak interaction effects for party and ideology could also be due to measurement error in these items. As discussed earlier and in the appendix, the party and ideology measures are purged of election results and demographic characteristics

Table 5.1 INTERACTION EFFECTS BETWEEN STATE CHARACTERISTICS AND MEASURES OF PERCEIVED AND ACTUAL ELITE POLARIZATION ON STATE-LEVEL PRESIDENTIAL OUTCOMES, 1972–2012

Independent Variable	T-score for Interaction with Specified Independent Variable			
	Perceived Candidate Difference	Perceived Party Distance	Important Party Differences	Congressional Polarization
Net Democratic Identification	-4.81	-.88	1.63	.84
Net Liberal Identification	2.10	2.00	2.70	2.72
% Advanced Degrees	5.56	5.29	5.42	6.98
% Foreign-Born	5.33	5.44	5.37	7.21
% Union	2.36	-.27	.21	.22
Congregation per10,000	-5.15	-6.03	-6.16	-7.72
% Single	3.17	3.44	4.56	5.10

NOTE: All interaction effects were estimated from a pooled data set (1972–2012) with a random-effects regression model using standardized independent and dependent (Democratic share of the two-party vote) variables. All models included controls for presidential and vice-presidential home-state advantage and southern regional controls for the Carter and Clinton candidacies. **Bold** = p < .05.

that are typically used to anchor such variables at the state level (Berry et al. 2010; Enns and Koch 2013; Pacheco 2011).

Additional evidence of a broader influence of the partisan context can be found in the correlations between the overall fit of the model used to produce Figure 5.6 and the level of elite polarization over time. The correlations between congressional polarization and model fit over time are .73 for the full model, .75 for the demographic model, and .76 for the party and ideology model

THE MULTIVARIATE MODEL

The results in Figure 5.6 tell us how well a group of variables explains state outcomes but do not tell us anything about how well individual variables perform when considered alongside other variables in a single model. As I noted before, many of these variables are highly correlated with each other, and their explanations of state election outcomes no doubt overlap with each other. This means that many of the bivariate relationships presented in Figure 5.4 may not emerge in quite the same way in a model that includes a set of highly correlated variables. Indeed this turns out to be the case for some variables. For instance, when party, ideology, percent foreign-born, percent advanced degrees, union membership, congregations per 10,000, and percent single are entered in the same model (along with home state and regional controls used previously), important variables such as percent advanced degrees and percent foreign-born produce much different results.[11] Table 5.2 presents the multivariate model for three different time periods. (See the appendix for election-specific results.) For percent advanced degrees, the slope is negative in the 1970s and 1980s and positive in the later time periods but is never close to statistically significant. And the slope for percent foreign-born has no significant influence on election outcomes throughout the data series, though it is negative and almost significant (using a two-tailed test, since the slope is opposite of expectations) in the 1984–88 and 2004–12 periods. These null results are not terribly surprising, especially for these variables, given their

Table 5.2 STATE CHARACTERISTICS AND PRESIDENTIAL OUTCOMES IN THE
STATES, 1972–2012

	1972–80	1984–88	1992–2000	2004–12
	b/s.e.	b/s.e.	b/s.e.	b/s.e.
Net Democratic Identification	0.072	*0.293*	*0.485*	*0.271*
	0.103	0.087	0.093	0.076
Net Liberal Identification	**0.329**	0.185	0.029	**0.241**
	0.188	0.225	0.128	0.115
% Advanced Degrees	−0.14	−0.108	0.057	0.084
	0.149	0.17	0.116	0.08
% Foreign-Born	0.037	−0.196	−0.05	−0.108
	0.124	0.1	0.064	0.066
% Union	*0.243*	*0.35*	**0.179**	0.078
	0.096	0.128	0.079	0.074
% Single	*0.331*	*0.429*	0.129	**0.215**
	0.109	0.142	0.09	0.1
Congregations per 10,000	−0.047	−0.026	*−0.355*	*−0.287*
	0.133	0.173	0.125	0.1
Presidential Home State	**0.185**	0.045	*0.169*	*0.071*
	0.097	0.068	0.05	0.026
Vice-Presidential Home State	0.113	**0.076**	0.069	**0.116**
	0.071	0.039	0.029	0.052
South 1976–80	*0.656*			
	0.106			
South 1992–96			−0.05	
			0.076	
Constant	0	0	0	0
	0.079	0.096	0.065	0.055
N	150	100	150	150
R^2	0.531	0.51	0.728	0.789

(*continued*)

Table 5.2 CONTINUED

	1972–80	1984–88	1992–2000	2004–12
	b/s.e.	b/s.e.	b/s.e.	b/s.e.
Adjusted R^2	0.497	0.461	0.708	0.776
RMSE	0.704	0.731	0.537	0.47

NOTE: All models estimated with clustered (by state) standard errors. **Bold** = p < .05; ***bold italics*** = p < .01 (one-tailed); and b/se = slope/standard error. The dependent variable is the Democratic share of the two-party vote. All variables are standardized (mean = 0, S = 1) within each year. The independent variables are described in the text and in the appendix.

interconnectedness with other variables in the model. For instance, throughout the entire time period percent foreign-born and percent advanced degrees were highly correlated with each other (r =.60); percent foreign-born was also correlated with net liberal (r =.48), union membership (r =.48), percent single (r =.64), and congregations per capita (r = −.72); and percent advanced degrees was correlated with net liberal (r =.58), percent single (r =.59), and congregations per 10,000 (r = −.68). The connections to cultural variables point to important explanations for why these variables matter so much in the bivariate patterns and perhaps also in the dynamic analysis in chapter 4. Parts of the country with higher levels of educational attainment and a greater proportion of people born in other countries tend to be associated with nontraditional, culturally liberal social and political outcomes. In the case of education, it is possible that less traditional states produce more people with advanced degrees, but it is also possible that people with advanced degrees are attracted to and migrate to less traditional states. Of course the foreign-born population is not "produced" in any state, so it is more likely that culturally progressive states are greater magnets for the foreign-born population.

Among the other substantive variables, familiar patterns emerge. Ideology mattered more than party early on; party was more important from 1984 to 2000; and both party and ideology were important explanatory variables from 2004 to 2012.[12] It is interesting that union membership played an important role up through the 2000 election, and percent single was an important influence in all periods except 1992–2000. But one of the more interesting patterns is that for religious congregations per capita, which was not statistically significant up through the 1988 election but was negative and statistically significant from 1992 to 2012. In fact judging importance of impact based on the coefficients (standardized within years), congregations per 10,000 was second only to net Democratic identification from 1992 to 2000 and had the greatest impact (slightly edging out net Democratic identification) from 2004 to 2012.

Taken together the evidence from Table 5.2 and from the preceding figures leaves little doubt that an important change has taken place, a change in the structure of state-level presidential election outcomes. Across a whole variety of influences, including standard state demographic, cultural, and political characteristics, correlations with state-level election outcomes have increased in magnitude. As a consequence, state-level outcomes are more predictable, signaling that there is more structure to those outcomes. Notably some of the factors that have taken on more importance in the past couple of decades—religiosity, party identification, and political ideology—are exactly the types of influence that one might expect to be activated by increasingly distinct political parties.

DO CHANGING RELATIONSHIPS MATTER?

A fundamentally important question yet to be answered is how much it matters that relationships have changed over time, that state outcomes are more connected to state characteristics now than in the past. By "how much it matters," I mean how would outcomes today be different if the basic statistical relationships observed for elections from decades ago had not changed? Consider the 2012 election. Given the state characteristics— party, ideology, advanced degrees, foreign-born, union membership, percent single, and religious congregations—and how they are related to the state outcomes that year, how different might we expect those outcomes to have been if the "predictions" for the 2012 election were based on slopes from the 1972–80 model? This is a bit trickier than trying to assess how changes in the values of state characteristics are related to changes in elections outcomes, as we did in chapter 4. Here we can observe differences in relationships and model fit over the years, but it is difficult to assess how—or even if—those changes had an impact on election outcomes. Part of the problem is the fact that even the estimates for a given year, based on data from that year, do not perfectly predict the actual election outcomes, so changes in predicted outcomes are not the same thing as changes in actual outcomes. Still, in any given year the estimated outcomes based on state characteristics do summarize our best guess at how those characteristics affect outcomes.

The strategy I use is to compare outcomes in a given year, predicted by the values of state characteristics and slopes for that year, to outcomes using the same values for state characteristics, but this time substituting slopes from a different time period. The difference in these estimates can then be interpreted as the expected gains or losses from one period to the next based on differences in relationships. This is summarized more formally in Equation 5.1, using estimated Democratic gains if the relationships in 2012 were the same as those for the period 1972–80.[13]

$$Democratic\ Gain_i = \sum_{k=1}^{K} \beta_k^{(2012)} X_{i,k}^{(2012)} - \sum_{k=1}^{K} \beta_k^{(1972-80)} X_{i,k}^{(2012)} \qquad (5.1)$$

First, for each state, i, sum the product of the 2012 values of the independent variables times their corresponding 2012 slopes across all K independent variables. The sum of those products equals the predicted state outcome in 2012 based on the 2012 relationships and state characteristics. The predicted 2012 state outcomes based on 1972–80 slopes are similarly obtained by summing the products of the 1972–80 slopes times the 2012 values for each corresponding independent variable.[14] The difference between these two estimates is a rough estimate of the extent to which the changes in the relationships favored Democratic (positive difference) or Republican (negative difference) interests.

A couple of examples might help illustrate how this works. Based on the 2012 regression estimates, the predicted 2012 outcome in Massachusetts was for Democrats to garner 66% of the two-party vote, about 4 points greater than their actual margin. However, substituting the slopes from the 1972–80 model, but still using 2012 values of the independent variables, generates a prediction of 54% of the two-party vote. The difference between these two estimates—12 percentage points—is interpreted as an estimate of the extent to which Democrats have gained strength in Massachusetts as a result of the changes in the underlying relationships between state characteristics and election outcomes. At the other end of the spectrum, the 2012 model estimates that Democrats would win 48% of the two-party vote in Alaska, about 5 points higher than their actual margin, while the prediction based on slopes form the 1972–80 model (using 2012 values of state characteristics) is for a Democratic victory with 55% of the two-party votes. The difference between these two predicted outcomes (–8 points) suggests that Democrats lost considerable strength in Alaska due to the changes in the relationships between state characteristics state outcomes. As I said earlier, these are rough estimates of how the parties have been affected by changes in relationships and should be taken as such. The best way to interpret these estimates is perhaps not as precise estimates of exactly how much the parties have gained or lost but relative to each other. So, for instance, we can say that Democrats benefited in Massachusetts but lost ground in Alaska due to changes in the structure of state election outcomes.

To get a general sense of how changing relationships have affected party fortunes, I focus on the three most recent elections—2004, 2008, and 2012—and examine how the parties benefited or were hurt by changes in the pattern of influences between two historical periods, 1972–80 and 1984–88, and each of the three more contemporary elections. In each of the comparisons measures of potential change are created using the formula in Equation 5.1. As might be anticipated, all the expected outcomes changed somewhat for all states when substituting coefficients from different periods. However, many of the changes were quite small, while others were substantial in magnitude. In order to gain a better sense of the extent of important change, I focus on those states in which the effect of changes in relationship moved the state at least 4 points in the Democratic or Republican direction. In Table 5.3 these states are listed in order of magnitude in each cell; states that were affected in a consistent direction across all three elections in a given row are in bold italics, and states that were consistently affected in two elections are in bold. Several patterns emerge from this table. First, most of the fifty states do not meet the sensitivity criterion of change in predicted outcomes of at least 4 points.[15] Considering the top two rows (changes from 1972–80 slopes), on average only twelve states in any given election cycle met the 4-point criterion. In the bottom two rows (changes from the 1984–88 slopes) the number of states affected by changes in slopes (4 points or greater) was only slightly higher, averaging just about fourteen per election cycle. Second, although it varies somewhat from year to year, there are roughly equal numbers of states moving in the Republican and Democratic directions. Third, for the most part the changes produced by differences in relationship match up with many of the actual changes in party support observed in chapter 1. Alaska, Montana, North Dakota, Utah, and West Virginia are among those states consistently identified as having moved in the Republican direction by changes in slopes and are in fact states whose actual outcomes moved considerably in the Republican direction from the early 1970s to the 2010s. Colorado, Connecticut, Delaware, Florida, Maryland, Massachusetts, New Hampshire, and Virginia are consistently identified as being pushed in the Democratic direction by changing relationships and are also states that have in fact moved in the Democratic direction over the past four decades. Fourth, there are a few "misplaced" states (Hawaii, Illinois, Mississippi, and Texas) whose change in predicted outcome is in the opposite direction of their actual movement. In some cases this could be an indication that the actual movement of these states over time—perhaps due to compositional changes—might have been even greater if not for the effects of changing relationships, which pulled in the opposite direction and constrained their movement somewhat. This notwithstanding, most of the influences on states in Table 5.3 make sense, pointing to changing relationships as a potentially important source of political change.

Table 5.3 STATES WITH THE GREATEST POTENTIAL CHANGE IN PARTISAN STRENGTH RESULTING FROM CHANGES IN RELATIONSHIPS BETWEEN STATE CHARACTERISTICS AND DEMOCRATIC VOTE SHARE IN PRESIDENTIAL ELECTIONS

		2004	2008	2012
Change from 1972–80 Slopes	Helped Republicans	ND, SD, MS, *AK*, WY, MT, **UT**, CA	*AK*, IL, ND	*AK*, IL, WV, AL, **UT**
	Helped Democrats	*MD*, TX, *NH*, *CT*, RI, VT, **DE**	DE, *MD*, *CT*, *NH*, VA, AZ, CO, MA	MA, *NH*, *MD*, *CT*, CO
Change from 1984–88 Slopes	Helped Republicans	*AK*, ND, *MS*, *WV*, SD, MT	*AK*, *WV*, *MS*, MI, HA	*AK*, *WV*, KY, AL, *MS*, MT, HA, MI
	Helped Democrats	*FL*, *NH*, *VA*, *CT*, MD, *CO*, AZ, MA, TX	*CO*, *FL*, DE, *VA*, *NH*, *CT*, VT	*CO*, *FL*, *NH*, *VA*, *CT*, ID

NOTE: States listed in this table are those whose estimated change in presidential vote share due to changes in relationships between election periods (see Equation 5.1) was at least 4 points in either direction. States are listed in order of magnitude of change. States in ***bold italics*** appear in the same row in all three election years; those in **bold** appear in the same row in two years; and those in roman appear in one year.

REVISITING CHANGES IN STATE CHARACTERISTICS

The preceding analysis has shown that changes in the national political context are connected to important changes in the relationships between state characteristics and state outcomes and that those changes in relationships have an impact on outcomes. Yet it is difficult to get a handle on the relative importance of changing relationships versus changing state population characteristics, at least with the data presented thus far. The analysis presented in chapter 4 demonstrated the importance of changing characteristics, but it is difficult to compare directly the strength of those findings to the results of the analysis presented in this chapter, given that the two approaches are very different from each other. However, the strategy used in this chapter to evaluate the impact of changing relationships can be modified slightly to generate comparable estimates of the impact of changing state characteristics on state outcomes. For instance, suppose we are interested in estimating the impact of demographic change from 1972 to 2012.[16] In this case (Equation 5.2) we can first estimate the predictions for 2012 using 2012 slopes and 2012 population characteristics, just as we did in Equation 5.1. Next we can estimate the 2012 outcomes still using 2012 slopes, but now substituting state demographic characteristics from 1972. The difference in these two estimates is an approximation of how different the 2012 election might have been if the composition of the state population (relative to other states) had not changed since 1972. Put another way, the difference in predicted outcomes can be used as an estimate of how much changing population characteristics affected changes in outcomes.

$$Democratic\ Gain_i = \sum_{k=1}^{K} \beta_k^{(2012)} X_{i,k}^{(2012)} - \sum_{k=1}^{K} \beta_k^{(2012)} X_{i,k}^{(1972)} \qquad (5.2)$$

Similar to the analysis of changing relationships, the effects of changing population composition are presented in Table 5.4, again listing states in which the difference in predicted outcomes was at least 4 percentage points in either party's favor. The first difference to emerge is that there are many more states in Table 5.4 that meet the 4-point threshold than there were in Table 5.3. Whereas roughly a dozen states met this criterion in either of the two groupings in Table 5.3, almost half—twenty-seven for 1972 characteristics, on average, across the three elections, and twenty, on average, for the 1984 population values—meet the criterion in Table 5.4. I take this as an indication that the effects of changes in state characteristics are much more widely felt—have a substantial impact on many more states—than are the effects of changes in relationships. Even a cursory visual inspection of the two tables gives the impression of much stronger effects from changes in population characteristics than from changing relationships. One way to think about the impact of the two different forms of change is to consider overall how much the predicted outcomes changed when slopes or characteristics from other periods are substituted for the actual slopes and characteristics. For instance, comparing the average absolute change in predicted outcomes attributable

Table 5.4 STATES WITH THE GREATEST POTENTIAL CHANGE IN PARTISAN STRENGTH RESULTING FROM CHANGES IN THE VALUES OF STATE CHARACTERISTICS

		2004	2008	2012
Change from 1972–80 State Characteristics	Helped Republicans	*WY, MS, AL,* *LA, SC,* **TX,** *UT, MT,* GA, NV, OK, NM, *WV*	*WY, AL,* SD, AK, *MS, UT,* *LA, WV,* NE, KS, *MT,* KY, MA, TX, *SC,* TN	*UT, WY, MS,* NE, *WV, AL,* WI, *MT,* MO, *LA,* TN, AK, KS, ID, MA, SC
	Helped Democrats	*NH, VT, RI,* MA, *ME, NY,* IA, *IL, ND,* MD, CT, DE, *OR,* WI	MD, DE, *VT,* NH, IL, ND, CA, RI, NY, CT, *ME, OR,* HA	MD, *NH,* CA, NY, *VT, IL, RI,* CT, *OR, ND,* ME, AZ, FL, WA
Change from 1984–88 State Characteristics	Helped Republicans	*MS, WY, AL,* NV, TX, *WV,* SC, **GA,** MT, WA, **KY**	AL, AK, *MS,* NY, *WY,* KY, LA, *WV,* KS, NV, SD	*MS,* UT, *AL,* *WY,* WI, **GA,** AK, *WV,* MT
	Helped Democrats	RI, *NH,* HA, DE, MA, ND, *VT,* ID, IA, NY, WI	DE, *VT,* IL, HA, TX, CA, ND, *NH,* MA, RI	CA, *VT, NH,* IL, CT, SD, OR, NM, **TX,** AZ

NOTE: States listed in this table are those whose estimated change in presidential vote share due to changes in state characteristics between election periods (see Equation 5.2) was at least 4 points in either direction. States are listed in order of magnitude of change. States in ***bold italics*** appear in the same row in all three election years; those in **bold** appear in the same row in two years; and those in roman appear in one year.

to each source can capture the relative impact of compositional change versus changes in relationships. Taking change in slopes first, the average absolute change (across the three election cycles) in predictions was 2.5 points using the 1972–80 slopes, and 3.1 points using the 1984–88 slopes. Using compositional change, the average absolute change (across the three election cycles) in predictions was 5.5 points using the 1972 characteristics and 4.0 points using the 1984 characteristics.[17]

CONNECTING CHANGES IN ESTIMATES WITH CHANGES IN OUTCOMES

Perhaps the most important way to judge the substantive importance of estimated changes in model predictions is to compare those changes to changes in actual outcomes. If changes in actual outcomes can be explained by the changes in estimated outcomes produced by manipulating characteristics and relationships, then we are on firmer ground in claiming that changes in characteristics and relationships produce changes in outcomes. Tables 5.2 and 5.3 suggest that predicted Democratic gains (losses) generally occurred in states where Democrats experienced gains (losses) in actual vote share, but the nature of the tables makes it a bit difficult to gauge with any degree of precision just how closely predicted gains and losses track with actual gains and losses. We can get a clearer picture of this by using a simple regression model in which changes in actual election outcomes from one period to another are regressed on the changes in estimated outcomes that were the product of differences in state characteristics and relationships. In Table 5.5 the base periods for changes in vote shares are the mean Democratic proportion of the two-party vote in 1972–80 and 1984–88, and change in vote share is measured by taking the difference between these two periods and the individual state election outcomes in 2004, 2008, and 2012. The independent variables are the measures of changes in predicted outcomes resulting from changes in relationships and state characteristics, as described earlier and summarized in Tables 5.2 and 5.3. The slopes for these variables summarize the extent to which changes in actual outcomes are connected to changes in underlying relationships or changes in state characteristics.

The results in Table 5.5 are pretty clear on two points. First, differences in predicted outcomes based on changes in state characteristics and regression slopes between time periods track well with changes in actual election outcomes. Generally speaking, states in which Democrats were predicted to increase (decrease) their vote share due to changes in characteristics and relationships are states in which their actual vote share increased (decreased). On average, the model explains about 47%

Table 5.5 THE RELATIONSHIP BETWEEN CHANGES IN ESTIMATED
OUTCOMES BASED ON DIFFERENCES IN SLOPES AND DIFFERENCES IN STATE
CHARACTERISTICS AND CHANGES IN ACTUAL ELECTION OUTCOMES

Change in Democratic Vote Share from 1972–80 Average

	2004	2008	2012
Change in Estimated Outcome Due to Changes	0.133	0.16	0.189
in Slopes	0.187	0.265	0.307
Change in Estimated Outcome Due to Changes	*0.646*	*0.86*	*0.789*
in Characteristics	0.103	0.131	0.139
Constant	*0.033*	*0.084*	*0.062*
	0.006	0.008	0.009
N	50	50	50
R²	0.508	0.508	0.459
Adj. R²	0.487	0.487	0.436
RMSE	0.044	0.058	0.065

Change in Democratic Vote Share from 1984–88 Average

	2004	2008	2012
Change in Estimated Outcome	*0.729*	0.359	**0.687**
Due to Changes in Slopes	0.171	0.227	0.267
Change in Estimated Outcome	**0.365**	*0.623*	**0.643**
Due to Changes in Characteristics	0.132	0.168	0.211
Constant	*0.044*	*0.095*	*0.073*
	0.006	0.008	0.009
N	50	50	50
R²	0.41	0.375	0.384
Adj. R²	0.385	0.348	0.358
RMSE	0.045	0.058	0.063

NOTE: The dependent variable is the difference in the Democratic share of the two-party vote between each election (column heading) and the specified election period average. The independent variables are the difference between the predicted outcomes in each election cycle based on contemporaneous slopes and state characteristics and the predicted outcomes in each election cycle when slopes (Equation 5.1) or state characteristics (Equation 5.2) from the other election periods are substituted.

of the variance in change in outcomes with 1972–80 as the baseline and 38% with 1984–88 as the baseline. The model does not capture all of the change in votes, but it is clear that a significant share of that change is connected to differences in expected outcomes that result from changes in state characteristics and changes in the relationships between those characteristics and vote share. This supports the argument that changes in votes respond to both changes in state characteristics and changes in the relationships between those characteristics and votes.

The second important finding—one that jibes with the differences between Tables 5.2 and 5.3—is that changes in state characteristics are much more important than changes in relationships. The slopes for changes in predicted outcomes due to state characteristics are positive and significant in every model, while changes in predicted outcomes due to differences in slopes are significant in only two of the six models. It is interesting to speculate why change in slopes from the 1972–76 period did not matter as much as changes in slopes from the 1984–88 period. One potential explanation is that an important variable throughout the 2004–12 elections was state political ideology, which was also important during 1972–80 (in the pooled model, upon which the comparisons are based). Perhaps, then, the differences in slopes between 1972–80 and the three contemporary elections was not great enough to produce significant differences in prediction, whereas the differences from the 1984–88 slopes were great enough to help shape differences in outcomes. This points to an important consideration: there could be limits to the potential for contextual effects to produce radically different outcomes, unless the alteration of the political environment is truly substantial in magnitude, such that the underlying relationships are not just altered but are genuinely transformed. This is not to say that the effects noted here (important contributions to change from the 1984–88 period) are not substantively important, just that they pale in comparison to the effects of compositional change. There are important changes in the pattern of relationships over time—in particular the increased salience of party and ideology, along with the sudden and sustained salience of religious congregations per capita beginning in 1992—but these changes have not produced concomitant changes in state outcomes to nearly the same degree that have been produced by changes in state characteristics.

SUMMARY

The U.S. political landscape has undergone a significant and well-documented change in the past several decades. Whether measured by the legislative behavior of members of the House of Representatives, the U.S. Senate, or sitting presidents, the ideological polarization between Democratic and Republican elites grows wider and wider with time. Notably this increase in polarization has not happened in a vacuum, and the general public has picked up on it, to the point where they now perceive the parties as more distinct ideologically and are more likely to cite important party differences than at any other point since modern measurement of these concepts began. The objective of this chapter was to estimate the impact these changes have had on state-level presidential election outcomes. Based on the contextual model spelled out in both this chapter and chapter 2, the expectations were that increased elite polarization would facilitate the connections between state demographic and political characteristics and election outcomes and that these heightened relationships would play a role in altering outcomes over time.

The evidence shows quite clearly that the relationships between most state characteristics and election outcomes have changed considerably over time. In most cases the magnitude of the relationships jumped around a bit in the 1970s and 1980s, perhaps in response to election-specific stimuli, and then grew increasingly strong throughout the 1990s and 2000s. It is interesting that the turnaround point for most of these relationships was somewhere around the 1988 or 1992 elections. This rough point of demarcation has been noted by others studying related issues. Writing about the partisan connection to abortion attitudes among the mass public, Andrew Gelman (2015, 91) quipped, "On or about 1990, as a latter-day Virginia Woolf might say, American politics changed."[18] Gelman's point was about the individual-level relationship between attitudes toward abortion and party identification, but the same could be said about the pattern of aggregate relationships shown in this chapter. Whether looking at individual variables or the overall fit of a multivariate model, key demographic and political variables are more strongly related to and provide a better statistical explanation of state outcomes in the 1990s and 2000s than in the 1970s and 1980s.

The key question for this analysis, however, is whether these changes in relationships had an impact on election outcomes. As anticipated, changes in the relationships between independent and dependent variables have some impact on changes in party strength in the states. However, the magnitude of these effects is somewhat limited. First, depending on the base years of comparison, generally fewer than half of the states (on average, about fifteen in any given year) registered effects in either direction of at least a 4-point shift in predicted vote. Second, these effects generally pale in comparison to the impact of changes in state characteristics, which produced shifts in estimated vote changes of at least 4 points in just about half the states in any given election year. Shifting context produces interesting changes in the pattern of influences on state election outcomes, and those changes have some effect on the outcomes themselves, but it is changes in state characteristics that have the greatest potential to alter the political landscape of U.S. presidential elections.

Demographic and Political Change

This book was motivated by two related propositions, each of which attracted increased attention with Barack Obama's election in 2008 and gained credibility with his reelection in 2012, almost to the point of becoming conventional wisdom. The first proposition is that there has been a shift in power over time that resulted in something like a Democratic lock on the Electoral College, that Democrats have built winning margins in the right combination of states to put Republicans at a significant and potentially long-term disadvantage. The second proposition, typically offered as an explanation for the shifting balance in the Electoral College, is that changes in state demographic characteristics—in particular changes in the racial and ethnic composition of key states—have moved some states from the Republican to the Democratic column. Evidence presented in the preceding chapters shows that while there is some truth to both propositions, the full story is a lot more complicated, nuanced, and, frankly, interesting.

There has indeed been an apparent shift in the relative strength of the two major parties in the Electoral College. From 1972 to 1988 Republicans won the presidency in four of five elections, but won only two of the next six elections between 1992 and 2012. As telling as the wins-losses comparison is between these two periods, the differences are not necessarily indicative of shifting strength in the Electoral College nor of changes in the geographic bases of party support. In fact a comparison of the two eras suggests that the Republican Party's main problem has been its inability to muster enough popular votes to gain an edge in electoral votes. However, this does not rule out changes in built-in party advantages in the Electoral College, changes that could make it more difficult for the Republican Party to win the electoral vote in close elections. In fact this is exactly what was shown in the analysis of hypothetical Electoral College outcomes in close popular vote contests (chapter 1). What had once been a slight Electoral College advantage for Republicans in simulated 50/50 outcomes has changed to a slight Democratic advantage in the past several election cycles. What's more, what was once a substantial Republican electoral vote margin in scenarios in which their share of the national two-party vote was 51% has dwindled to a very small advantage. By this account, there has been a change in the relative power of the two major parties, but something more along the lines of a tremor than a seismic shift. To be sure, Democrats are better positioned now than they have been in the past several decades, but their position is best characterized as a slight advantage rather than an electoral lock.

By contrast, if you look under the hood, so to speak, at changes in party strength in the states, the movement over time has been truly substantial for many states, and the net impact of shifting state loyalties is such that it could certainly produce the observed changes in the Electoral College. Changes in party support in the states flowed in several directions: some states moved sharply in the Republican direction, some sharply in the Democratic direction, some moved less dramatically, and a few barely moved at all. A few overall patterns seemed to benefit Democratic presidential candidates. Although there were nearly equal numbers of states moving in each direction, the number of electoral votes associated with states that moved Democratic far outstripped the number associated with states that moved Republican. The same pattern exists in states that are more consequential to Electoral College outcomes, those states whose competitive status has changed over time. Another pattern that could benefit Democrats, at least in terms of making gains in new territory, is that most of the Republican gains over the past several decades have been in states where they already enjoyed an advantage. This pattern of consolidation stands in stark contrast to the experience of the Democrats, whose gains were made mostly in previously competitive or Republican states, representing a tendency toward penetration rather than consolidation. Implications of this difference are explored later in this chapter.

WHAT EXPLAINS CHANGE?

Shifts in party support across the states don't just happen; there are forces in play, both among the states and in the country as a whole, that help shape the way states change politically over time. There are two very broad categories of influence on the states: compositional effects and contextual effects. Compositional effects are based on changes in state demographic and political characteristics. Contextual effects are based on how the broader national context alters the way state characteristics are connected to state outcomes. The argument for compositional change as a source of political change is straightforward. Over time states have experienced substantial and substantively important changes in the composition of their populations, and those changes have led to transformations of the political orientation of many states. States that experienced relatively greater growth in Republican-aligned groups, or declines in Democratic-aligned groups, generally increased their level of support for Republican presidential candidates, while states that experienced relatively high levels of growth among Democratic-aligned groups generally boosted their level of support for Democratic presidential candidates. The argument concerning contextual effects is a bit more complicated. The basic proposition is that the national political context has changed in important ways—primarily related to increased ideological polarization among party elites—and those changes have activated, or facilitated, the connection between group characteristics and party support. If you think of state outcomes as a function of the levels of some set of population characteristics, weighted by some values that translate those characteristics into political outcomes, then contextual changes affect outcomes by altering the weights.

EVIDENCE OF COMPOSITIONAL EFFECTS

Multiple important compositional effects on changing political outcomes emerged in this book, primarily in chapters 3, 4, and 5. Migration patterns, including both internal (state-to-state) and foreign-born migration, have had a profound effect on changes in state political disposition. Generally states in which the percentage of the CVAP who were foreign-born increased the most over time tended to be states in which Democrats made important gains. Part of this effect is related to how this variable moves with other variables. In particular there is a strong relationship between changes in the foreign-born population and changes in the percentage of the population who are nonwhite. In part this reflects changes in the racial and ethnic composition of the foreign-born population, which was dominated by European immigrants in the 1970s and is now dominated by Asian and Latin American immigrants. In terms of internal migration, the key influence is not whether states have high or low levels of internal migrant population but rather where those migrants came from. States that tend to draw internal migrants primarily from liberal states tend to move in the Democratic direction, while those that draw from conservative states move in the Republican direction. This effect is amplified if the internal migrant population constitutes a substantial part of the state population.

Another important demographic source of change is the percentage of the population with an advanced degree. In fact in bivariate and multivariate models in chapter 4 this emerged as one of the most consistently important influences on changes in state outcomes. States that saw relatively large increases in percent advanced degrees were also states that shifted most dramatically Democratic, and states with the lowest growth in percent advanced degrees shifted most dramatically Republican. Changes in rates of advanced degrees also had important effects on changes in party identification and changes in ideology at the state level, as did changes in union membership and changes in the poverty rate. It should be noted that, just as change in the foreign-born population was picking up some of the effects of changes in the racial and ethnic composition of the states, change in rates of advanced degrees is picking up some the influence of changes in occupational status (percent professional) in the states. Changes in the size and geographic concentration of professionals as a population group have previously been tied to changes in Democratic prospects (Bishop 2009; Judis and Teixeira 2004), and those findings receive support here. However, changes in level of education prove to be more closely tied to political outcomes.

The importance of changing population characteristics received additional support in the analysis of population characteristics in chapter 5, which did not focus on the role of individual characteristics but on how changes in a group of characteristics—party, ideology, union membership, percent advanced degrees, percent foreign-born, percent single, and religious congregations per 10,000 population—contributed to changes in state outcomes by simulating those outcomes based on population characteristics from other time periods. Generally states whose populations changed in ways that would augur for greater Democratic (Republican) success were also states whose outcomes moved in the Democratic (Republican) direction. Taken together, these findings point to population change as an important source of political change.

EVIDENCE OF CONTEXTUAL EFFECTS

The contextual model required several things to happen over time: increased ideological polarization among party elites, heightened public perceptions of increased party polarization, increasingly strong relationships between state characteristics and state election outcomes, and changes in state outcomes as a result of changes in relationships. There was strong evidence on the foundational pieces of the contextual model, and there is some evidence that changes in context resulted in changes in outcomes, but that evidence is not nearly as strong as evidence of the importance of compositional changes. There is little doubt that Republican and Democratic elites have become more polarized over time, as evidenced by roll call voting data presented here. It is also clear that the public picks up on this increased polarization, as perceptions of party differences show a widening gulf in the perceived positions of the parties. Most important there is strong evidence of a changing pattern of relationships between state demographic and political characteristics and presidential election outcomes in the states. When viewed in isolation, the relationships between each of nine separate state characteristics and Democratic support followed a similar pattern: the magnitude of the relationship bounced around a bit in the 1970s and 1980s but steadily increased in strength from 1992 to 2012. A similar pattern was found in the multivariate analysis, where the explanatory power of the model increased steadily over time beginning in the 1980s. An examination of interaction effects showed that the impact of most state characteristics was conditioned by both the level of elite polarization and public perceptions of elite polarization.

All of the pieces are in place, then, to produce changes in state outcomes that can be traced to changes in the underlying relationships between state characteristics and state outcomes. And there is evidence that this is what happened. When simulating how outcomes from 2004 to 2012 would have been different if the relationships had not changed since the 1970s or 1980s, there were a number of states in which Republicans benefited from the change in relationships from other periods and a number of states in which Democrats benefited. Generally speaking, the states in which Republicans were expected to make their largest gains were also states where they actually made gains, and the same was true for Democrats. However, these effects are much more limited than the effects that emerged when estimating how different the outcomes were due to changes in demographic characteristics. Changes in demographic characteristics produced substantial effects in nearly twice as many instances as was the case for changes in relationships, and the relationship between expected and actual change in outcomes was much stronger for changing demographics than for changing relationships. Both dynamics have been at play, but changing relationships are less potent than changing demographics.

RELATED CONSIDERATIONS

Before wrapping things up, I address two important issues that help explain what has happened and some of the implications of these findings for the future of presidential elections. First, I revisit the pattern of vote distribution across the states to assess the potential for changing patterns to lead to inefficiencies for the Republican Party. Then I look forward in time to the implications of the preceding analyses for the 2016 and future elections.

REVISITING PATTERNS OF CHANGE

One of the interesting patterns of vote change observed in chapter 1 was the tendency for Republicans to make their gains in areas where they already had a relative advantage, even if just leaning Republican, whereas Democrats tended to make their gains in previously Republican or competitive states. One implication of this pattern is that Republicans may be consolidating their votes into fewer and already Republican states, whereas Democratic votes may be more geographically diverse, resulting in narrower Democratic victories but in the right combination of states. On one hand, consolidation could be viewed as a plus for Republicans, as they have more states they can bank on in any given election year. Barring a lopsided Democratic popular vote, adding to built-in vote advantages in more states could be an advantage to Republicans. Of course that is if those states represent a proportionate number of electoral votes. On the other hand, the Republican distribution of votes could be very inefficient, generating lower Electoral College returns per vote, giving Democrats an advantage because their votes are more evenly distributed.

One way to look at this is to simply count as solid wins the number of states in which a party wins a substantially greater share of the vote compared to its national vote share, and see if that count has grown for either party over time. The standard I use here is whether the Democratic or Republican Party had a margin 10 points greater than its national vote margin in any of the states. So, for instance, in a dead-heat national popular vote election, a state in which the outcome was 45/55 would be counted for the winning party as a solid win (+10-point margin compared to national vote). By this method both parties have increased the number of states in which their margins are solid, but Republicans have outpaced Democrats slightly. From 1972 to 1984 there were eight solid Democratic and thirteen solid Republican states, on average, and from 2000 to 2012 those numbers increased to fourteen solid Democratic and twenty solid Republican states, on average. Republicans have held an edge in this category throughout the time period, but the value of that edge is somewhat illusory when the electoral votes of the solid states are taken into account. For instance, the average electoral vote total of solid Republican states from 1972 to 1984 was 82, compared to 78 for Democrats, a virtual tie. From 2000 to 2012, despite holding an edge in number of states, the solid Republican states represented 163 electoral votes, on average, compared to 182 electoral votes, on average, for solid Democratic states. This suggests an increasing relative inefficiency in the distribution of Republican votes across the states.

One concept related to the efficient allocation of votes is that of wasted votes (Ardoin 2009; Pattie and Johnston 2014; Stephanopoulos and McGehee 2015). By the standard definition, any votes received by a party in excess of the number required to win a state (or legislative district, as this concept is usually applied to legislative contests) is a wasted vote, as are all votes received by a party in states in which the party loses. Every state-level outcome will generate a lot of wasted votes, but the key point is that if Party A is running up the margins in a number of states, and Party B is winning by narrower margins in other states, Party B has a more efficient distribution of votes. This is particularly important if the two parties are of roughly equal strength in the population, in which case running up the margins in a handful of states leaves Party A less able to compete effectively in the remaining states. Interestingly, inefficient allocation of votes in U.S. House races is widely seen as a problem that plagues the Democratic rather than the Republican Party. In House races Democrats tend to be concentrated ("packed," to use a gerrymandering term) into fewer, mostly urban districts in which they win by wide margins, but then find themselves spread too thin to provide serious competition in the majority of remaining districts (Jacobson 2012). This problem with efficiency has plagued congressional Democrats since the mid-1990s and has grown more severe over time (Stephanopoulos and McGehee 2015).

We can assess the trend over time in the relative efficiency of Republican to Democratic vote distributions by taking the ratio of Republican wasted votes to Democratic wasted votes in each year. High values of this ratio indicate greater Democratic efficiency, and low values indicate greater Republican efficiency. Figure 6.1 presents the data on relative efficiency. Here we see an almost complete bisection of the data series in which Republicans held an advantage in vote efficiency (values less than 1) from 1972 to 1988, while Democrats held an advantage from 1992 to 2012, lending some support to the idea that the Republican challenges in the Electoral College may be tied to changes in the distribution of votes across the fifty states. There also appears to be a connection between winning and relative efficiency. Republicans won every election in which they had the more efficient allocation of votes and lost five of the seven elections in which Democrats were more efficient, though interparty differences in efficiency in 2000 and 2004 were relatively slight.

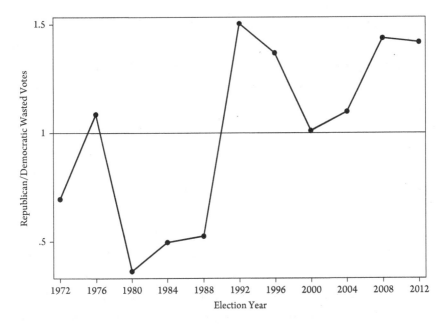

Figure 6.1 Relative Efficiency of Vote Distributions (High Values Favor Democrats) in U.S. Presidential Elections, 1972–2012

NOTE: Wasted votes are defined as every vote cast for a party in states in which the party loses and every vote in excess of the number of votes need to win in states in which the party wins.

Republicans tend to hold solid advantages in more states compared to Democrats, but without gaining an overall electoral vote advantage. This pattern suggests a Republican problem with efficiency, and the data on wasted votes support this idea, at least for the past several election cycles. Of course the inefficiency is a problem only if it has a real connection to winning or losing elections, which is in keeping with the data I presented. In addition Pattie and Johnston (2014) identify party differences in vote allocation efficiencies as one of the primary determinants of bias in the Electoral College. It is difficult to tell if this pattern will persist into the future, but if it does, it will continue to be a problem for Republican prospects.

THE 2016 ELECTION AND BEYOND

It is interesting to speculate about the ramifications of the findings presented in this book for both the short-term and long-term strength of the two major parties. Certainly it seems reasonable to assume that the patterns uncovered here should have some continued impact on future elections. However, it is important to understand that the analysis in this book is an attempt to describe and explain what has happened over a forty-year swath of electoral history and is not designed or intended to provide precise forecasts of future election outcomes. Still it is possible to look at the likely relative positions of the states in the 2016 election, generate some educated guesses about the Electoral College outcomes based on alternative popular vote scenarios, and highlight important demographic trends that might push some of the swing states in one direction or another.

In the absence of a strict forecasting model for state outcomes, the best we can do this far out from the election (summer 2015) is use past outcomes as a guide for likely patterns in 2016. The data in Table 6.1 are based on a weighted average of the state outcomes from the 2004–12 presidential elections, assigning the most weight to 2012 and the least to 2004.[1] The first column of data in Table 6.1 shows the average Democratic vote share centered on the Democratic share of the national two-party vote. So, for instance, Utah has a value of –22.9, which means that, on average, Democrats run almost 23 points behind their national vote share in Utah. In a dead-heat national contest, the expected Democratic share of the two-party vote in Utah would be 27%. With this information we can calculate the expected Democratic vote share in each state based on hypothetical values of the national two-party vote. The expected winners, based on the vote estimates, are indicated with an R (Republican) or a D (Democrat) in the last four columns of the table. Using these simple estimates we can arrive at some projections of the expected number of electoral votes, given the hypothetical national vote outcomes.[2]

An important point to glean from these electoral vote estimates (Table 6.1) is one I made in chapter 1: If candidates take care of their national vote margin, they will more than likely win the Electoral College vote as well. However, a couple of bits of data reinforce the slight Democratic advantage. Let's start by looking at the expected outcomes and then examine the potential for some of the swing states to change those outcomes. In the event of a Republican victory with 52% of the two-party vote, the Republican candidate would end up with 311 electoral votes, 41 more than needed to win. Looking at the states standing between this expected outcome and a potential Democratic upset, Democrats could try to pick up the friendliest states: Nevada, Pennsylvania, New Hampshire, Iowa, and Colorado (listed most to least likely). This is not completely implausible, but it would mean running the table in all of the states they need and not losing any states they are expected to win. Another possibility is that Democrats could just pick up the electoral vote–rich states of Pennsylvania and Florida to win with 276 electoral votes. Pennsylvania is somewhat plausible, but Florida would be a stretch, with an expected Democratic vote there of 46.5% of the two-party vote. Bottom line, if Republicans win 52% of the two-party national vote, they almost certainly win the election.

The Electoral College outcome with a Republican popular vote victory of 51% of the two-party vote is a bit less certain. The Republican nominee would still be expected to win, but with 275 electoral votes, only 5

Table 6.1 Projected 2016 Electoral College Outcomes under Alternative Popular Vote Margins

State	Democratic Vote	Electoral Votes	Hypothetical Two-Party National Vote				
			52% R	51% R	50%	51% D	52% D
Utah	−22.9	6	R	R	R	R	R
Wyoming	−20.5	3	R	R	R	R	R
Oklahoma	−18.0	7	R	R	R	R	R
Idaho	−17.6	4	R	R	R	R	R
Alabama	−13.2	9	R	R	R	R	R
Nebraska	−12.7	5	R	R	R	R	R
Arkansas	−12.1	6	R	R	R	R	R
Kansas	−12.1	6	R	R	R	R	R
Kentucky	−12.0	8	R	R	R	R	R
West Virginia	−12.0	5	R	R	R	R	R
Alaska	−11.4	3	R	R	R	R	R
Tennessee	−10.7	11	R	R	R	R	R

State	Democratic Vote	Electoral Votes	Hypothetical Two-Party National Vote				
			52% R	51% R	50%	51% D	52% D
North Dakota	−10.7	3	R	R	R	R	R
Louisiana	−10.6	8	R	R	R	R	R
Texas	−9.7	38	R	R	R	R	R
South Dakota	−9.7	3	R	R	R	R	R
Mississippi	−8.6	6	R	R	R	R	R
Montana	−7.5	3	R	R	R	R	R
South Carolina	−7.4	9	R	R	R	R	R
Arizona	−6.4	11	R	R	R	R	R
Georgia	−6.1	16	R	R	R	R	R
Indiana	−6.0	11	R	R	R	R	R
Missouri	−4.8	10	R	R	R	R	R
North Carolina	−3.3	15	R	R	R	R	R
Florida	−1.5	29	R	R	R	R	D
Virginia	−0.5	13	R	R	R	D	D

(continued)

Table 6.1 CONTINUED

State	Democratic Vote	Electoral Votes	Hypothetical Two-Party National Vote				
			52% R	51% R	50%	51% D	52% D
Ohio	-0.5	18	R	R	R	D	D
Colorado	0.7	9	R	R	D	D	D
Iowa	1.2	6	R	D	D	D	D
New Hampshire	1.3	4	R	D	D	D	D
Pennsylvania	1.5	20	R	D	D	D	D
Nevada	1.8	6	R	D	D	D	D
Minnesota	2.2	10	D	D	D	D	D
Wisconsin	2.3	10	D	D	D	D	D
New Mexico	3.3	5	D	D	D	D	D
Michigan	3.7	16	D	D	D	D	D
Oregon	4.5	7	D	D	D	D	D
Washington	5.5	12	D	D	D	D	D
Maine	5.8	4	D	D	D	D	D
New Jersey	5.8	14	D	D	D	D	D

State	Democratic Vote	Electoral Votes	Hypothetical Two-Party National Vote				
			52% R	51% R	50%	51% D	52% D
Connecticut	7.2	7	D	D	D	D	D
Illinois	7.6	20	D	D	D	D	D
Delaware	7.8	3	D	D	D	D	D
California	9.1	55	D	D	D	D	D
Maryland	10.2	10	D	D	D	D	D
Massachusetts	10.6	11	D	D	D	D	D
New York	11.4	29	D	D	D	D	D
Rhode Island	11.7	4	D	D	D	D	D
Vermont	15.3	3	D	D	D	D	D
Hawaii	17.4	4	D	D	D	D	D
District of Columbia	40.7	3	D	D	D	D	D
Total Electoral Votes			311 R	275 R	272 D	303 D	332 D

NOTE: The first column of data shows the average centered (on the national popular vote) Democratic vote share using a weighted average of the state outcomes from the 2004–12 presidential elections. The second column of data indicates the number of electoral votes at stake in each state in 2016. The main body of the table indicates the expected winner (D = Democrat, R = Republican) in each state based on alternative national popular vote scenarios.

votes to spare. In this case all the Democrats would have to do is pick up Colorado to reach 272 electoral votes and they could pile on by picking up Virginia and Ohio, both of which are within reach. What makes this particularly intriguing is that Colorado and Virginia are two states in which certain key population characteristic have been trending in the Democratic direction. From 2000 to 2012 Virginia was among the ten states in which the foreign-born population and professional class were growing the fastest, and Colorado was one of the ten states with the fastest growing populations with advanced degrees. Ohio seems like more of a long shot for Democrats, in part because it has trended very, very slightly in the Republican direction in the past three elections. Of course any Democratic chance of victory requires that they hold Iowa, New Hampshire, Pennsylvania, and Nevada. The most vulnerable among these are probably New Hampshire and Pennsylvania, where the 2004 Democratic presidential candidate John Kerry outperformed the national Democratic vote by wider margins than Barack Obama did in both 2008 and 2012. The bottom line, though, is that at 51% of the national two-party vote, the Republican nominee will hold a narrow but vulnerable advantage. Recall from chapter 1 that one of the important trends in expected electoral votes was that Republican candidates in the 1980s and 1990s were very secure with 51% of the vote, but that advantage had dwindled appreciably by 2012.

In a toss-up popular vote election, the Electoral College is a virtual toss-up as well, though Democrats hold the narrowest of advantages, with an expected total of 272 electoral votes. If Republicans pick up any of the expected Democratic states, they win. However, this assumes that Democrats don't at the same time pick up any Republican states. What makes victory a bit more difficult for Republicans is that if they manage to pick up an additional 19 electoral votes by winning Colorado, Iowa, and New Hampshire—all plausible—Democrats could still win by picking up 18 votes in Ohio, which is equally plausible. And if Democrats also pick up Virginia or, less likely, Florida, Republicans would have virtually no chance of winning. In fact if you look at the states in play in a 50/50 outcome, Democrats have many more electoral votes within reasonable reach than do Republicans. In a 50/50 contest Democrats have a slight edge, though one that could certainly be overcome.

The odds begin to shift significantly toward a Democratic victory if Democrats win 51% of the two-party vote. In this scenario Democrats improve upon their 50/50 outcome by picking up Ohio and Virginia, ending up with an expected 303 electoral votes. This Democratic edge could be a bit tenuous, as they would be expected to barely win in Virginia and Ohio. But at the same time Republicans would have to pick up Ohio, Virginia, and Colorado and not lose any of the states they are expected to win (Florida seems most vulnerable) in order to pull off an upset. If Democrats win 51% of the national two-party vote, they certainly have an easier path to 270 than Republicans do if they win by the same popular vote margin. At 51% of the national vote, Republicans have a cushion of 7 electoral votes, while Democrats have a cushion of 33. Neither of these margins is a sure thing, but the Democratic margin seems more certain. Again this highlights the fact that Republicans are more vulnerable now with narrow popular vote margins than they were forty years ago.

In the event that Democrats win 52% of the national two-party vote, they add Florida to their column and end up with an impressive 332 electoral votes. In this scenario a Republican path to victory seems very difficult, requiring that they pick up Florida, Virginia, Ohio, and Colorado, while not losing any states they are expected to win. (It seems unlikely that Democrats would pick up either North Carolina or Missouri.) Of these states, Florida is the most likely Republican pickup, but the others seem pretty unlikely. At 52% of the national two-party vote, it seems highly likely that Democrats carry the Electoral College.

A key takeaway point from these patterns is that in a close national vote outcome (50/50 or 51/49), Democrats have a slight edge heading into the 2016 election. Given that a Republican vote of 51% provides only a small electoral vote advantage, leaving them only slightly safer than Democrats with 50% of the national vote, and that Democrats appear to be relatively safe with 51% of the national vote, the advantage goes to the Democratic Party. Having said this, anything outside this narrow range of popular vote outcomes will almost certainly result in an Electoral College victory for the winner of the popular vote. A substantial popular vote victory is the best Electoral College strategy for either party.

There are a couple of things to note before moving on from this discussion. First, there is a relatively small group of states that fall within this 4-point range from a 52% Republican victory to a 52% Democratic victory. These states—Florida, Virginia, Ohio, Colorado, Iowa, New Hampshire, Pennsylvania, and Nevada (listed from least to most likely for the Democrats)—represent a likely core of what will be battleground states in the 2016 campaign. None of these states should surprise political observers, as they are habitually on battleground lists. Moving out from these states in either direction are other states that have experienced intense campaigning in recent presidential elections, including North Carolina, Minnesota, Wisconsin, and New Mexico. Second, as mentioned earlier, these estimates are being made without any information about how the presidential campaign unfolds between now (summer 2015) and the general election campaign, including who ends up as the presidential and vice-presidential nominees. As it happens, there are several people from the current pool of presidential candidates who hail from some of the swing states: two from Florida, two from Virginia, and one each from Ohio, Pennsylvania, and Wisconsin. Should either ticket end up with a presidential candidate from one of these states, it could upset the Electoral College apple cart. It is also possible that either ticket could end up with a vice-presidential candidate from one of the swing states, which could also alter the likely outcome in close elections.

Additionally race and ethnicity could play out in interesting ways that have implications for the Electoral College. Without President Obama on the Democratic ticket, it seems reasonable to expect African American support for the Democratic ticket to drop from the almost unanimous levels of 2008 and 2012 to the just really high levels (around 90%) from previous elections, and also that African American turnout could wane a bit. Among the swing states in Table 6.2 this has the greatest potential to affect outcomes in Virginia, Florida, Ohio, and Pennsylvania (listed from highest to lowest black percentage of CVAP). At the same time, it is possible that there could be offsetting effects, as Democratic support among

Table 6.2 SUMMARY OF CHANGES IN KEY POPULATION CHARACTERISTICS, 2000–12

Lowest Growth in Non-White Population	Lowest Growth in Foreign-Born	Most Conservative Shift in Internal Migration	Lowest Growth in Percentage Advanced Degrees	Lowest Growth in Percentage Professionals
Hawaii	Alaska	Alabama	Arkansas	Alaska
Kentucky	Hawaii	Connecticut	California	Delaware
Maine	Louisiana	**Florida**	**Florida**	Maine
Michigan	Maine	Hawaii	Indiana	Montana
Missouri	Mississippi	Kentucky	Louisiana	**New Hampshire**
New Hampshire	Montana	Massachusetts	Maine	North Dakota
South Carolina	**New Mexico**	Mississippi	Mississippi	South Dakota
Vermont	South Dakota	New Jersey	South Dakota	Texas
West Virginia	West Virginia	Oklahoma	West Virginia	Vermont
Wyoming	Wyoming	Vermont	Wyoming	Wyoming

(continued)

Table 6.2 CONTINUED

States in Which Population Changes Favor Democratic Prospects

Greatest Growth in Non-White Population	Greatest Growth in Foreign-Born	Most Liberal Shift in Internal Migration	Greatest Growth in Advanced Degrees	Greatest Growth in Professionals
Arizona	California	**Colorado**	**Colorado**	Arkansas
California	**Florida**	Delaware	Connecticut	**Colorado**
Connecticut	Georgia	Idaho	Maryland	Connecticut
Delaware	Maryland	**Nevada**	Massachusetts	**Iowa**
Florida	Massachusetts	New Mexico	**New Hampshire**	New Jersey
Georgia	**Nevada**	**North Carolina**	New Jersey	**North Carolina**
Maryland	New Jersey	Oregon	North Dakota	Oklahoma
Nevada	New York	Rhode Island	Oregon	Tennessee
New Jersey	**Virginia**	South Carolina	Rhode Island	**Virginia**
Texas	Washington	Texas	**Virginia**	West Virginia

NOTE: All population characteristics are based on the CVAP.

whites could have been softened a bit due to the unique racial circumstances of 2008 and 2012. Equally interesting is the prospect of a Latino candidate, either at the top of the Republican ticket (Senators Ted Cruz of Texas and Marco Rubio of Florida are both running for the Republican nomination at this writing) or as the vice-presidential nominee for either party. Democrats have seen important increases in support among Latino voters over the past several elections, and blunting that advantage in key swing states (New Mexico, Florida, Nevada, and Colorado, in order of Latino CVAP) could improve Republican chances in a close election.

BEYOND 2016

If it is risky to offer insights into likely outcomes in 2016, it is certainly more risky to predict elections further out in time. Instead I look at trends in key population characteristics over the past few election cycles and identify states in which the trends favor one party over the other. Based on these trends, we can get a sense of the potential for either party to realize gains in relative strength in the future. Rather than assess every characteristic that was examined in the preceding chapters, I focus on a few that have been shown to be particularly important here and elsewhere (Bishop 2009; Judis and Teixeira 2004). Table 6.2 summarizes changes in a number of key characteristics across the states from 2000 to 2012. This is a much narrower period of change than was used earlier in the book, so the magnitude of change is much smaller than, say, from the 1970s to the 2000s. This is also a more contemporary perspective and has the benefit of looking at the rate of change that is likely to persist into the near future. Table 6.2 lists the ten states whose rate of change on each of the five characteristics have most favored Republican growth and the ten states whose rate of change most favored Democratic growth. To the extent that states' changing populations consistently favor growth for one of the parties, it seems reasonable to expect that those are states where that party has the greatest potential for growth. Of particular interest here are potential swing states, those states in Table 6.1 for which a swing of just a few percentage points could tip the state to one party's column or the other. Those states are highlighted in bold in Table 6.2.

A couple of interesting patterns appear in Table 6.2. First, although there are some Democratic states with Republican-friendly population shifts and few Republican states undergoing Democratic population pressures, it is much more common to find that states in both camps tend to experience reinforcing population pressures. This could exacerbate the trend toward flatter distributions of state votes (see chapter 1), as states grow increasingly faithful to one party or the other. Second, population changes in swing states have a more Democratic than Republican bent. Of the twenty-one swing state outcomes in Table 6.2, only five are listed as favoring Republicans, while the other sixteen favor Democratic growth. Three swing states (Florida, New Mexico, and New Hampshire) have population changes in both directions, while a number of others experience multiple population changes in the Democratic direction. Colorado, Nevada, North Carolina, and Virginia stand out as having the clearest potential for future Democratic gains; should these states indeed swing Democratic, Republicans will find themselves in an increasingly difficult spot vis-à-vis the Electoral College. These patterns of demographic change reflect recent changes and could persist into the near future. If we assume that changing demography continues to shape election outcomes the way it has in the past, then the data in Table 6.2 do not offer much encouragement for improved Republican electoral prospects, especially in close popular vote elections.

DEMOGRAPHY AND DESTINY

"Demography is destiny" is an increasingly popular aphorism used to describe the assumed importance of the demographic makeup of electorates to the fate of political parties.[3] *Destiny* is a strong word, though, implying inevitability, and I doubt that most people who use it to describe politics mean it literally. However, if demography is not, strictly speaking, destiny, it certainly plays an important role in shaping the fate of political parties. The evidence presented in this book demonstrates important group-based connections to levels of party support and to changes in levels of party support in the states. As a group, a relatively small collection of demographic characteristics do a good job explaining changes in party support over forty years of political history. But there is nothing deterministic or inevitable about this relationship or its consequences for the parties. Although the general tendency is for states to support candidates as a function of their demographic composition, there is some slack in this relationship, with some states fitting the pattern better than others. More important, the relationship between state demographic composition and state election outcomes has changed over time, growing stronger in response to changes in what the parties represent, and it can certainly change in the future.

While the outlook for the Democratic Party does not vastly outstrip that of the Republican Party, the perception of looming demographic problems for Republicans is supported here. It is not so much that population groups whose numbers are on the rise favor the Democratic Party (though many of them do) but that the geographic distribution of changes in the size of key population groups have favored Democrats. Specifically Democrats have made more inroads into Republican and competitive states, in part due to changes in those states' populations, and there is some evidence to suggest a continuation of that pattern, at least in the short term. However, the die is not cast ... yet.

If changes in party positions can activate group-based connections to the parties, it is also possible that political parties can act to weaken those same connections. If groups such as immigrants, racial minorities, and those with a high level of education are put off by Republican policies and the geographic distribution of these groups has taken a toll on Republican prospects, then it is possible that Republicans can soften the blow of demography by changing the image, if not the policies, of their party. This is essentially the advice offered by some within the Republican Party who argue that the party needs to rethink its approach to race, immigration, climate change, and other issues that seem to put the party on the wrong side of growing population groups (Gluek 2014; Ladd 2014).

Parties can't control demographic trends, but through their policies and issue positions they may be able to affect how those characteristics translate into political support. To the extent that parties are able to influence how groups align for or against them, even if just at the margins, they are not defenseless in the face of demographic headwinds. Instead parties can help shape the extent to which demography is their destiny.

ELECTION OUTCOME DATA (USED THROUGHOUT)

All data for state-level presidential election outcomes are taken from David Leip's Atlas of U.S. Presidential Elections (http://uselectionatlas.org/). Data for state-legislative elections are taken from Carl Klarner's data website (https://dataverse.harvard.edu/dataset.xhtml?persistentId=hdl:1902.1/22519) and, for the 2012 election, from the National Conference of State Legislatures (http://www.ncsl.org/documents/statevote/legiscontrol_2013.pdf).

STATE-LEVEL POPULATION CHARACTERISTICS (USED THROUGHOUT)

Most of the state-level population characteristics were taken from U.S. census data, made available by Integrated Public Use Microdata (IPUMS), which can be accessed at https://usa.ipums.org/usa/. For elections from 1972–2000 the decennial census data were used (1% sample from Form 1 in 1970, and 1% samples for 1980, 1990, and 2000), and data from the annual American Community Survey were used for 2004, 2008, and 2012. Estimates for each election year between the census samples were generated from a linear interpolation. In 1970 estimates were missing for several states with a small population, including Delaware, Idaho, Montana, North Dakota, South Dakota, Vermont, and Wyoming. The values of each variable for these states were estimated based on the relationship between their 1980 values and the overall mean value of each variable in 1980. For instance, if the value for Delaware on a given variable was 2 points lower than the national average in 1980, the 1970 value would be estimated to be 2 points lower than the national average in 1970.

All data taken from IPUMS were measured relative to the citizen voting-age population, defined as those respondents who are at least eighteen years old and a U.S. citizen. Population characteristics measured directly with census data are percent advanced degrees, percent female, percent foreign-born, percent internal migrants (and their birth states), percent in poverty, percent professional occupation, race/ethnicity (percent non-Hispanic white, black, other, and percent Latino), and percent single.

Most of the categories for these variables are straightforward, but a few do require further explanation. For *percent professional*, 1990 occupational codes (occ1990) were used, and the following occupations are designated as professional: architects and engineers; mathematical and computer scientists; natural scientists; health diagnostic occupations; health assessment and treatment occupations; therapists; primary, secondary, and postsecondary teachers; librarians, archivists, and curators; social scientists; social, recreational, and religious workers; lawyers and judges; writers, entertainers, and athletes. For *poverty*, respondents were coded as living in poverty if their total family income was between 0 and 100% of the federally defined poverty level income for a family of their size (the IPUMS variable "poverty" was recoded for this purpose). For *advanced degrees*, the 1970 and 1980 census data (educ) identify years of schooling rather than degree earned, so advanced degrees is defined here as percentage of the population completing five or more years of college. *Internal migrants* were defined by matching current state of residence (statefip) with birthplace (bpl). People whose birthplace differed from their current state of residence and who were born in the United States or a U.S. territory were coded as internal migrants.

Data on a few population characteristics came from sources other than the census. Religious penetration measures (congregations per 10,000 population and religious attenders as a percentage of state population) were taken from the U.S. Religion Census (www.usreligioncensus.org), which provides estimates for 1971, 1980, 1990, 2000, and 2010. Data for years between these dates are estimated using linear interpolation, and the 2010 data are used for the 2012 election. The link to individual data reports is found at http://www.rcms2010.org/compare.php. Data for union membership are taken from Hirsch and MacPherson (2014) and represent the percentage of each state's nonagricultural wage and salary employees who are union members. Note that unlike estimates from census data, population estimates for the religion and union items are not based on the CVAP.

INDIVIDUAL-LEVEL MEASURES OF PARTY, IDEOLOGY, AND MOBILITY (CHAPTER 3)

Questions Used to Measure Respondent Party and Ideology

All GSS question wordings came from the online codebook (http://gss. norc.org/documents/codebook/GSS_Codebook_mainbody.pdf) and all ANES question wordings came from the ANES online codebook (http:// electionstudies.org/studypages/anes_timeseries_cdf/anes_timeseries_ cdf_codebook_var.pdf).

GSS ideology: "We hear a lot of talk these days about liberals and conservatives. I'm going to show you a seven-point scale on which the political views that people might hold are arranged from extremely liberal—point 1—to extremely conservative—point 7. Where would you place yourself on this scale?"

Scale values:

1. Extremely liberal
2. Liberal
3. Slightly liberal
4. Moderate
5. Slightly conservative
6. Conservative
7. Extremely conservative

GSS party identification: "Generally speaking, do you usually think of yourself as a Republican, Democrat, Independent, or what?"

IF REPUBLICAN OR DEMOCRAT: "Would you call yourself a strong (Republican/Democrat) or not a very strong (Republican/Democrat)?"

IF INDEPENDENT, NO PREFERENCE, OR OTHER: "Do you think of yourself as closer to the Republican or Democratic Party?"

Scale values:

0. Strong Democrat
1. Not strong Democrat
2. Independent, near Democrat
3. Independent
4. Independent, near Republican
5. Not strong Republican
6. Strong Republican
7. Other party

ANES ideology: "Here is a seven-point scale on which the political views that people might hold are arranged from extremely liberal to extremely conservative. Where would you place yourself on this scale, or haven't you thought much about this?" In 2000 "When it comes to politics do you usually think of yourself as extremely liberal, liberal, slightly liberal, moderate, or middle of the road, slightly conservative, extremely conservative, or haven't you thought much about this?"

Scale values:

1. Extremely liberal
2. Liberal
3. Slightly liberal
4. Moderate, middle of the road
5. Slightly conservative
6. Conservative
7. Extremely conservative

Questions to Determine Where Respondents Lived as Children

GSS: "In what state or foreign country were you living when you were 16 years old?"
ANES: "Where was it that you grew up? (IF UNITED STATES:) Which state or states?"

STATE PARTY IDENTIFICATION AND POLITICAL IDEOLOGY (CHAPTERS 4 AND 5)

Estimates of state party identification and state political ideology are adapted from the Enns and Koch (2013) data, collected from hundreds of national surveys representing hundreds of thousands of individual respondents to produce policy mood, party identification, and political ideology. For party identification and political ideology, Enns and Koch produced aggregate estimates for each state from 1976 to 2010. The process for producing these estimates utilizes multilevel regression with poststratification (MRP), an increasingly popular method in which individual survey responses are weighted (based on individual-level relationships) by state-level characteristics to produce aggregate opinion estimates. Others have used this technique to estimate state-level opinion outcomes (Lax and Phillips 2009; Pacheco 2011), though sometimes with mixed success (Buttice and Highton 2013). In the poststratification step Enns and Koch use state demographic characteristics (sex, race, age, education) and region and presidential election outcomes to generate the final estimates of state party identification and political ideology.

The original Enns and Koch estimates of percent liberal and percent conservative are used to create the net state ideology measure (1972–80) for internal migrant birth states (Equation 3.1). Since the Enns and Koch data span the period 1976–2010, the 1976 data are used for the 1972 election. This measure is very well suited to capturing the (lagged) political environment of the birth states of internal migrants, in part because it combines both public opinion data and (less directly) information from presidential elections, based on how those elections are related to public opinion. While Robinson and Noriega (2010) in their study on political change in the Mountain West used only election returns to measure the political tendencies of counties from which internal migrants moved, the Enns and Koch measure taps into a broader political context.

However, it is problematic to use the original Enns and Koch measure for other parts of the analysis that involve explaining change in election outcomes based on changes in state demographic and political characteristics. To get around this issue I measure state party and ideology based almost exclusively on the raw survey marginal percentages from the Enns and Koch data. By their nature these estimates involve a lot more noise than the MRP estimates, but they avoid the serious issues of endogeneity posed by the MRP estimates.

There are a few interesting wrinkles involved in using the raw survey data. For many small states there were a number of years without survey data, as well as a few cases where data in a particular year were implausible, probably due to small sample sizes. For state years in which there were no survey results or in which the outcomes for one of the categories was zero or 100% (or very close to that), the data were declared missing and values of party and ideology were imputed based on a modified version of the MRP estimates. This involved generating estimates for most of the observations for Alaska and Hawaii and only a couple of observations for each of several other small states (Delaware, Montana, Nevada, New Mexico, North Dakota, South Dakota, West Virginia, and Wyoming). In total 4.8% of the 1,785 state-year estimates were imputed, and 63% of the imputed values came from Alaska and Hawaii. The imputed values are based on a three-year moving average version of the Enns and Koch measure that excludes presidential votes in the poststratification stage but still uses state demographic factors. Peter Enns generously provided this alternative measure, as well as the raw survey data. Imputation was done in STATA 13, using the "mi impute" command, which generated ten imputed values for each missing observation. The average of these imputed values was used as the estimate of percent Democratic, percent Republican, percent liberal, and percent conservative in place of the missing values.

Once the imputed data were generated, I computed moving average estimates in order to smooth out some of the noise in the election year estimates. For all election years from 1980 to 2008, three-year moving averages were used. For the 1976 election, the raw data from 1976 and 1977 were averaged. Since there was no measurement of party and ideology prior to 1976, the two-year estimates for 1976 were also used for 1972. Because the data series ends in 2010, the 2009 and 2010 data were averaged and used to estimate state party and ideology in 2012. Once the moving average percentages were calculated, measures of net party identification (Democrat-Republican) and net ideology (liberal-conservative) were created.

Idaho had only a couple of missing data points, but it was clear that there was something amiss with the trend in the estimates of net ideology for Idaho. Based on the measures of change in net ideology (percent liberal minus percent conservative) averaged from 1972–80 to 2004–12, liberals increased their standing in Idaho more than in any other state, gaining 18 points, while the mean change across all states was –7.6 points. By contrast, using the modified MRP data (based primarily on demographic postestimation), liberals lost ground in Idaho, losing 7 points, while the average change in the MRP measure was –9.8 points. I find the MRP trend for Idaho much more plausible on its face. Throughout the analysis all ideology values for Idaho are the adjusted (utilizing demographics but not election results) three-year moving average MRP estimates.

PERCEPTIONS OF PARTY AND CANDIDATE DIFFERENCES (CHAPTER 5)

Data on perceptions of party and candidate differences come from the American National Election Studies Cumulative Data File (Stanford University and University of Michigan 2014). The following are specific items used to generate the aggregate trends:

Perceptions of party and candidate differences: "We hear a lot of talk these days about liberals and conservatives. Here is a seven-point scale on which the political views that people might hold are arranged from extremely liberal to extremely conservative. Where would you place [the Democratic/Republican presidential candidate] on this scale?"

Perceptions of Democratic and Republican Party differences: "We hear a lot of talk these days about liberals and conservatives. I'm going to show you (1996 AND LATER: Here is) a seven-point scale on which the political views that people might hold are arranged from extremely liberal to extremely conservative. Where would you place the [Democratic/Republican] Party on this scale?"

Scale values:

1. Extremely liberal
2. Liberal
3. Slightly liberal
4. Moderate, middle of the road
5. Slightly conservative
6. Conservative
7. Extremely conservative

For *perception of important party differences*: "Do you think there are any important differences in what the Republicans and Democrats stand for?"

Codes:

1. No difference
2. Yes, a difference
9. DK; depends (1972)

MEASURES OF ELITE IDEOLOGICAL POLARIZATION (CHAPTER 5)

Data on party ideological differences in roll call voting come from voteview.com, specifically the House (ftp://voteview.com/house_polarization46_113.dta) and Senate (ftp://voteview.com/senate_polarization46_113.dta) polarization files, and the "common space" DW-NOMINATE scores, which are based on both House and Senate roll call votes, for presidents (http://voteview.com/dwnomin_joint_house_and_senate.htm).

Table A.1 ELECTION-SPECIFIC REGRESSION ESTIMATES FOR THE CROSS-SECTIONAL MODEL USED IN CHAPTER 5

	Year					
	1972	**1976**	**1980**	**1984**	**1988**	**1992**
Variable	**b/s.e.**	**b/s.e.**	**b/s.e.**	**b/s.e.**	**b/s.e.**	**b/s.e.**
Net Democratic	−0.098	0.276	*0.296*	*0.402*	0.171	*0.435*
Identification	0.112	0.173	0.103	0.091	0.128	0.126
Net Liberal	0.091	0.212	*0.622*	0.14	0.245	0.201
Identification	0.274	0.269	0.179	0.184	0.499	0.15
% Advanced Degrees	0.207	**−0.376**	**−0.288**	−0.242	0.026	0.087
	0.15	0.177	0.121	0.176	0.196	0.165
% Foreign-Born	0.219	0.081	−0.221	−0.195	−0.177	−0.237
	0.198	0.142	0.116	0.117	0.139	0.127
% Union	*0.371*	0.138	0.135	*0.339*	**0.439**	**0.235**
	0.12	0.153	0.088	0.131	0.224	0.104
% Single	**0.269**	**0.27**	*0.387*	*0.535*	0.292	−0.002
	0.138	0.152	0.129	0.147	0.17	0.134
Congregations per	0.189	−0.042	−0.172	−0.087	0.071	*−0.487*
10,000	0.17	0.186	0.173	0.191	0.207	0.158
Presidential Home	0.176	*0.249*	**0.107**	0.079	0.062	0.192
State	0.181	0.088	0.05	0.11	0.11	0.116
VP Home State	0.152	0.058	**0.115**	−0.008	**0.206**	*0.16*
	0.112	0.101	0.068	0.053	0.088	0.018
South 1972–76		*0.423*	*0.351*			
		0.153	0.096			

(*continued*)

Variable	Year					
	1972	1976	1980	1984	1988	1992
	b/s.e.	b/s.e.	b/s.e.	b/s.e.	b/s.e.	b/s.e.
South 1992–96						−0.013
						0.123
Constant	0.00	0.00	0.00	0.00	0.00	0.00
	0.101	0.1	0.078	0.093	0.116	0.091
N	50	50	50	50	50	50
R²	0.58	0.606	0.756	0.647	0.448	0.672
Adj. R²	0.486	0.505	0.694	0.567	0.324	0.588
RMSE	0.717	0.704	0.553	0.658	0.822	0.642

Variable	Year				
	1996	2000	2004	2008	2012
	b/s.e.	b/s.e.	b/s.e.	b/s.e.	b/s.e.
Net Democratic	*0.559*	*0.474*	*0.401*	0.188	0.134
Identification	0.12	0.097	0.101	0.121	0.1
Net Liberal	−0.272	0.005	0.2	**0.306**	*0.460*
Identification	0.208	0.222	0.171	0.151	0.158
% Advanced Degrees	0.131	0.119	0.099	0.106	−0.036
	0.149	0.14	0.114	0.109	0.113
% Foreign-Born	−0.002	0.068	−0.19	−0.065	−0.087
	0.102	0.077	0.103	0.085	0.113
% Union	**0.202**	0.153	0.055	0.092	0.048
	0.101	0.096	0.107	0.097	0.094
% Single	**0.237**	0.097	0.162	**0.202**	*0.326*
	0.1	0.101	0.131	0.102	0.114
Congregations per	−0.272	*−0.298*	*−0.392*	−0.182	−0.238
10,000	0.147	0.11	0.154	0.123	0.125
Presidential Home	**0.15**	*0.134*	0.027	*0.097*	0.06
State	0.085	0.014	0.057	0.034	0.069

Table A.1 CONTINUED

Variable	Year				
	1996	**2000**	**2004**	**2008**	**2012**
	b/s.e.	**b/s.e.**	**b/s.e.**	**b/s.e.**	**b/s.e.**
VP Home State	**0.076**	0.024	0.016	**0.242**	0.147
	0.036	0.057	0.025	0.099	0.118
South 1976–80					
South 1992–96	−0.086				
	0.109				
Constant	0.00	0.00	0.00	0.00	0.00
	0.074	0.067	0.074	0.064	0.068
N	50	50	50	50	50
R^2	0.782	0.818	0.778	0.831	0.81
Adj. R^2	0.727	0.776	0.728	0.793	0.767
RMSE	0.523	0.473	0.522	0.455	0.482

NOTE: **Bold** = $p < .05$; ***bold italics*** = $p < .01$ (one-tailed); and b/se = slope/standard error. The dependent variable is the Democratic share of the two-party vote. All variables are standardized (mean = 0, S = 1) within each year.

CHAPTER 1

1. Data on unemployment and GDP are from the Bureau of Labor Statistics (http://data.bls.gov/timeseries/LNS14000000) and the Bureau of Economic Analysis (http://www.bea.gov/national/xls/gdpchg.xls). Data on presidential approval are from the Gallup Poll (http://www.gallup.com/poll/116500/presidential-approval-ratings-george-bush.aspx; http://www.gallup.com/poll/116479/barack-obama-presidential-job-approval.aspx).

2. One problem with starting in 1972 is that President Richard Nixon's landslide victory surely renders this election unique and hard to compare to others. However, similar criticisms could be made of virtually any of the other elections in this series, including the Watergate hangover and unique regional effects due to a Deep South candidate in 1976; the overwhelmingly negative international and economic context of the 1980 election; Reagan's landslide victory over Mondale in 1984; and the list could go on. The unique aspects of each election do not render them incomparable, especially in later analyses where the state outcomes are centered to take the national context into account. Instead varied national experiences provide a solid basis for being confident that the results can be generalized broadly.

3. Note that this is very similar to a method developed by Brookes (1960) and later used by Johnston et al. (2001).

4. Despite said bumpiness, the trends are very similar when the data are disaggregated to individual elections, just a little harder to visualize. For instance, in simulated 50/50 elections, Republicans would have won all but two (1972 and 1980) of the six elections from 1972 to 1996, but would have won only one (2000) of the five elections from 1996 to 2012.

5. Another alternative is to center the outcomes on the average state vote rather than the national popular vote. Doing so produces results very similar to those presented here. The primary difference is that centering on the average state outcome shows Democrats making somewhat more substantial gains than obtained when centering on the national vote share. In analyses of models used to explain change in centered Democratic votes, however, the two methods produce virtually

identical results. The key drawback to centering on the mean state outcome is that it is a bit more difficult intuitively to connect the mean outcome to national party performance. This is because the mean Democratic vote share across the states is typically about 2 percentage points higher than the Democratic share of the national vote. For instance, a mean state outcome of 50% of the two-party vote for Democrats typically would occur in a year in which Democrats garner only 48% of the national two-party vote. So what would appear to be a toss-up election based on the fifty-state mean would actually be one in which the Republican candidate carried the day with a 4-point margin.

6. The regional effect of Carter's candidacy is much stronger than that for Clinton's candidacy.

7. Returning to the issue of the starting and end points of these series, dropping 1972 or ending the series in 2004, prior to the Obama candidacies, generates very similar trends in party support for the states.

8. Data used for this part of the analysis comes from Carl Klarner's collection of state legislative elections data: http://www.indstate.edu/polisci/klarnerpolitics. htm. I supplemented Klarner's data to include the results of the 2012 state legislative elections, using data from the National Conference of State Legislatures (ncsl. org).

9. Evidence of its increased salience can be gleaned from Google Scholar searches. For the period 2000–2004, Google Scholar produced 1,500 hits for "political polarization," and for the period 2010–14 it produced 6,530 hits.

10. It should be noted that higher levels of geographic polarization are found using country-level data (Bishop 2009). This is not surprising, given the more compact and homogeneous nature of counties compared to states.

CHAPTER 2

1. As mentioned before, Vermont is a close call on this.

2. Though not exactly equivalent, the professional class discussed here is loosely analogous to or overlaps with the "new middle class" (Manza and Brooks 1999), the "mass upper-middle class" (Abramowitz and Teixeira 2009), and the "creative class" (Florida 2004).

3. The data on the racial and ethnic breakdown are real data on shares of the citizen voting-age population and come from the state of Maryland in 1972 and 2012, but the vote breakdowns across groups are hypothetical and used to illustrate how varying group size and strength of relationship can affect outcomes.

4. This does not mean the public has finely grained, detailed information on the intricacies of party policy positions. Certainly that would be at odds with what we generally know about the level of political knowledge among the mass public (Delli Carpini and Keeter 1997). Instead my assumption is that the public "gets it" in broad strokes, something analogous to gut-level rationality (Popkin 1994). In the case of race, for instance, the public could get the idea that Democrats grew more likely, and Republicans less likely, to support legislation promoting the rights of blacks, without knowing any specifics about civil rights–related legislation. And in the case of abortion, simply getting a sense that Republicans

are "pro-life" and Democrats "pro-choice" would greatly clarify party positions without any knowledge of specific party actions.

5.   It should be noted that another way to think of the contextual effects described here is as a form of *conversion*, whereby people (or groups) change preferences over time, most likely in response to changes in the national political context. Both the increased strength of the Republican Party in the South and the increased strength of the Democrats in the Northeast are generally attributed to some combination of conversion and generational replacement (Carmines and Stimson 1989; Knuckey 2009; Miller 1991).

6.   This is likely due, in part, to the connection between occupational status and level of education. Recent work by Feldman and Johnston (2014) has shown that while people with a high level of education tend to be economic conservatives, they do also tend to be relatively liberal on social and cultural issues. Education levels have also been tied to liberal positions on postmaterial issues such as environmentalism (Coan and Holman 2008; Liere and Dunlap 1980).

CHAPTER 3

1.   Data from the American Community Survey and other Census Bureau studies were obtained from Ruggles et al. (n.d.). More details on which data files were used in this book are provided in the appendix.

2.   This does not address the issue of those citizen voting age residents who are not eligible to vote, such as convicted felons, in some states (McDonald and Popkin 2001). Unfortunately gathering data on felon status by population subgroups over time is not feasible. Still CVAP is a better approximation of the likely electorate than simply using the voting-age population (Holbrook and Heidbreder 2010).

3.   This overall net conservative ideological placement reflects a long-term trend in people being more willing to identify as conservative than as liberal (Clawson and Oxley 2012), even when the Democratic Party is relatively popular or when policy tastes run in the liberal direction (Stimson 2004).

4.   Since the period averages are taken from linear predictions generated by the slopes in Figures 1.3 and 1.4, the relationships are exactly the same if the actual slopes are used as the dependent variable.

5.   I have saved the impact of short-term migration changes on short-term political changes for another day. This book is focused on longer-term political change.

6.   Enns and Koch (2013) use hundreds of thousands of responses from hundreds of surveys that include questions on party identification and ideology to estimate state partisanship and state political ideology. In this book I use a couple of different versions of the Enns and Koch measure, details of which are provided in the data appendix.

7.   This variable is constructed from one that asked respondents in which state they lived when they were sixteen years old, but the GSS only provides the regional identifier.

8.   As of this writing (spring 2015) the 2012 ANES responses for the question about where respondents grew up have not been released.

9. The correlation between historical regional ideological predisposition and the mean of the 7-point ideology scale for regional migrants is also a very robust .65 in the GSS data and .79 for the ANES data.

10. This is a simple model that focuses on just two independent variables. Other influences are considered in later analyses. One omitted variable that might occur to scholars of state politics is a regional control for southern states. As it happens, when a southern control variable is added to the model, it has no significant influence (t-score = –.45), suggesting that whatever uniquely southern pattern there is to political change is accounted for by immigration patterns.

11. Given that the scatter plots in Figure 3.2 reveal a somewhat curvilinear relationship, the model was also tested using quadratic terms for both variables (e.g., b_1*foreign born + b_2*foreign born^2). Neither of the squared terms was significant, nor were the two terms jointly significant (F-ratio =.21, p =.89).

CHAPTER 4

1. Moreover group characteristics continue to play an important role not just in voting studies but also throughout the discipline of political science. Some evidence of the relevance of groups to political science can be gleaned from the number of sections of the American Political Science Association with an explicit focus on group politics. Six of the forty-six sections focus on some aspect of group politics: Class and Inequality; Migration and Citizenship; Race, Ethnicity, and Politics; Religion and Politics; Sexuality and Politics; and Women and Politics Research.

2. http://www.cawp.rutgers.edu/sites/default/files/resources/ggpresvote.pdf.

3. Chaney et al. (1998) find that the growth of the gender gap in the 1980s was partly in response to women holding more pessimistic views of the economy and attaching greater weight to economic issues.

4. The 2012 ANES had both a face-to-face and an Internet sample, but the face-to-face sample does not include the measure of occupational status used here. The Internet sample was drawn from the universe of eligible voters and included both pre- and postelection interviews, with an overall sample size of 3,860. The sampling weight designed for the Internet sample was used in this analysis.

5. One concern with these measures of socioeconomic status is that they overlap a lot with race and ethnicity (whites are more likely than nonwhites to have high income, high level of education, and professional occupation), so these simple estimates might overstate the relationship. However, when the analysis is restricted to white voters, the same general patterns of support appear for income and occupation (though all levels are less likely than nonwhites to vote Democratic), and for education those with advanced degrees stand out from all other groups as the most likely (.60) to vote for Obama.

6. The ANES demographic group breakdowns are taken from http://electionstudies. org/nesguide/2ndtable/t9a_1_1.htm. Exit poll results are taken from the Roper Center, http://www.ropercenter.uconn.edu/polls/us-elections/how-groups-voted/.

7. In previous ANES surveys it was possible to get finer affiliation distinctions. As of this writing, those finer distinctions are not yet available for the 2012 study.

8. Nonwhites constitute, on average throughout the time period studied here, 23% of the CVAP in southern states and only 16% in nonsouthern states.

9. If change is measured by first centering all of the variables on their mean levels at different points in time—so that, at each point in time, the variable is measured as how far above or below the fifty-state average a given state is—the regression slopes and correlations presented in this chapter stay exactly the same. The only thing that changes is the constant term in the regression models.

10. Data for this variable are taken from unionstats.com (Hirsch and MacPherson 2014) and represent the share of the percentage of each state's nonagricultural wage and salary employees who are union members. Note that this is not based on the CVAP.

11. One-tailed tests are appropriate here, given that positive trends are expected in both cases.

12. These data were collected by the U.S. Religion Census (www.usreligioncensus. org), which provides estimates for 1971, 1980, 1990, 2000, and 2010. Data for years between these dates are estimated using linear interpolation, and the 2010 data are used for the 2012 election. The link to individual data reports is at http://www.rcms2010.org/compare.php.

13. The set of variables explored above, and the narrower set explored below, surely do not exhaust all possible demographic influences. Data were gathered on several other indicators, including percent single female, percent white male, percent with less than twelve years of education, percent between the ages of eighteen and thirty, percent in creative, supercreative (Florida 2004), and managerial occupations. The list could go on and on, but it really shouldn't. In the end these additional indicators add nothing of substance—either because their effect is already capably picked up by other variables or because they just bear no relationship to votes—and including them, and other variables, would only serve to offend my (and probably the readers') parsimonious sensibilities and clutter up the analysis.

14. Collinearity at extreme levels can lead to substantially inflated standard errors for the slope estimates—increasing the likelihood of concluding that there is no relationship when in fact there is one—and, in some cases, sign switching of coefficients that makes no sense and results in theoretically perverse conclusions.

15. Both attendance and number of congregations are based on responses to surveys of religious organizations. My sense is that it is easier for those organizations to provide more accurate estimates of the number of congregations in their state than the number of regular attenders.

16. Returning to the issue of overlap between change in professionals and change in percentage with advanced degrees, there is more evidence that including change in professionals adds nothing to the model. When change in professionals is added to the model, it is not statistically significant, but change in advanced degrees remains significant and also remains the most important variable. When advanced degrees is dropped from the model and professionals replaces it, change in professionals is statistically significant, but the overall fit of the model drops off appreciably (adjusted $R^2 = .34$).

17. As I pointed out earlier, all states saw an increase in the size of the nonwhite population.

18. The tolerances for change in nonwhite percentage and change in foreign-born percentage are .20 and .22, respectively.

19. In a model including just the migration variables, both change in internal and foreign migration were statistically significant (slopes 11.48 and .90, respectively) and the model-adjusted R^2 was .39. The standardized coefficients indicate that internal migration ($\Delta Y, S_x$ = 3.32) is slightly more important than foreign-born migration ($\Delta Y, S_x$ = 2.47).

20. By contrast, the fit for the model is diminished if change in foreign-born is dropped in favor of change in percent nonwhite (R^2 drops to .59 and adjusted R^2 drops to .53).

21. Peter Enns very generously provided raw survey percentages, as well as various versions of the poststratified measure he created with Julianna Koch.

22. One of those nine states with an increase in net liberalism is North Dakota, which brings up an important point: an increase in net liberal identification doesn't necessarily mean a state is more liberal than conservative—just that the balance has changed somewhat in the direction of liberal identification. For instance, net liberal identification in North Dakota moved from −23 (a 23-point disadvantage) in the 1970s to −21 (a 21-point disadvantage) in the 2000s. This registers as a gain in net liberal identification, but North Dakota is by no means a liberal state.

23. When considered in isolation in bivariate models, the regression slope for change in party identification was .19 and that for ideology was .39. The fact that party affiliation loses strength and significance means that there is significant overlap between these two variables. Indeed the correlation between changes in party affiliation and ideology at the state level is .65.

24. It should be noted that change in internal migration is significantly correlated with both change in party identification (r =.39) and ideology (r =.48) in bivariate models. However, these effects are washed away when change in advanced degrees (which is correlated with change in internal migration) is entered in the model.

CHAPTER 5

1. For all presidents prior to Eisenhower, this measure is based on presidential requests to Congress.

2. Standard DW-NOMINATE scores are used for the House and Senate estimates and were obtained from voteview.com. Presidential scores are based on the "common space" DW-NOMINATE scores, which combine presidential preferences on both House and Senate roll call votes. More details on data sources are provided in the appendix.

3. See voteview.com, in particular the graphics pertaining to historical trends in polarization: http://voteview.com/images/polar_housesenate_difference_2014.png.

4. This assumes exposure through the mass media. Levendusky (2009) demonstrates that beginning sometime in the late 1980s, there was an increasing tendency for the media to focus on ideological polarization among party elites.

5. The data for this figure were generated using data from the ANES Cumulative Data File. Details on question wording are in the data appendix. All three of the

lines are estimated using lowess smoothing, which cuts down on the year-to-year
noise and summarizes the trend in the data.

6. Perhaps as an indicator of the low salience of political ideology, the ANES did
    not ask questions about respondent ideology or perceptions of candidate or party
    ideological placement prior to 1972.

7. This is based on "common space" DW-NOMINATE scores and includes com-
    parison to all Democratic candidates with a score from their record in Congress
    or as sitting president. The Democratic candidate in 1988, Massachusetts gover-
    nor Michael Dukakis, is not included in the comparison since he has no legisla-
    tive or presidential record.

8. These lines are lowess estimates, again intended to capture the trends in the data.

9. Because these are simple bivariate relationships they are not strictly the same as
    the relationships displayed in Figure 5.4, which are based on partial correlations
    controlling for home-state advantage and southern regional effects during the
    Carter and Clinton candidacies. Still the pattern of relationships is very similar to
    that found in Figure 5.4, and the individual scatter plots provide a nice glimpse of
    how those relationships evolved. In the case of religious congregations per 10,000,
    the relationship between the partial correlations and Figure 5.4 and the simple
    correlations for the plots in Figure 5.5 is .95.

10. The adjusted R^2 provides a basis for comparing how well models with different
    numbers of independent variables explain statistical variation in the dependent
    variable. The demographic model includes percent foreign-born, percent union
    members, percent advanced degree, percent single, and religious congregations
    per capita. The party and ideology model includes net Democratic identification
    and net liberal identification. All models include controls for presidential and
    vice-presidential home-state advantage, and a southern regional control for the
    Carter and Clinton candidacies is included for 1976–80 and 1992–96, respectively.

11. As in previous multivariate models, percent nonwhite and percent professionals
    are not included in the cross-sectional model due to overlap with percent foreign-
    born and percent advanced degrees, respectively.

12. It should be noted that the effects of net ideology in particular might be ham-
    pered a bit by collinearity (overlap) with the other independent variables. For
    the model from 1972–80, 45% of the statistical variation in net ideology was
    accounted for by the remaining independent variables, 61% from 1984—88, 55%
    from 1992–2000, and 70% from 2004–12. These are not dangerously high levels of
    collinearity but do represent a problem that does not affect net Democratic iden-
    tification, which had shared variances of 6%, 28%, 49%, and 24%, respectively, in
    these time periods.

13. The 1972–80 slopes are from Table 5.2, and the individual year estimates are in
    the appendix.

14. The dependent and independent variables are standardized within each election
    year so they have a mean of zero and a standard deviation of 1, which facilitates
    this calculation. If unstandardized variables were used, both the mean and the
    variance of each variable would fluctuate from year to year, as would the constant
    term of each regression model. This would make it difficult to use slopes from one
    election to estimate outcomes using data from another year and would lead to

implausible outcomes. Because the means and standard deviations of each variable are the same across election years, the slopes can be used to simulate the impact of changing slopes on outcomes. For each year the standardized predictions can be adjusted by the mean and standard deviation of the dependent variable in that year to transform them into raw predicted vote shares.

15. The average absolute change in predictions was 2.5 points using the 1972–80 slopes and 3.1 points using the 1984–88 slopes.

16. For looking at demographic change, single years are used as anchor points, since the demographic characteristics are fairly stable over a couple of election cycles, whereas regression slopes tend to bounce around a bit more.

17. In a similar vein the correlation between the simulated and election-year predictions can provide some insight into how different outcomes might have been in 2004–12 if different state characteristics or relationships had existed. The average correlation between the estimates based on simulations using different regression slopes and the election-year predictions is .90, while the correlation between estimates based on differences in state characteristics is .70. In other words, the estimates based on different slopes do not differ from the election-year estimates as much as the estimates based on different state characteristics do. This means that changes in slopes are less likely than changes in characteristics to produce estimates that are at great variance from the estimate produced by the election-year models.

18. This same pattern can also be found in Bafumi and Shapiro's (2009) examination of the partisan and ideological connections to cultural and social welfare issues.

CHAPTER 6

1. Specifically the weighted measure is ((2004 outcome+(2*2008 outcome)+(3*2012 outcome))/6). Virtually identical results are obtained if an unweighted average is used.

2. I use the term *simple* to emphasize that these estimates are based only on past voting patterns and do not incorporate any additional information that might make them as accurate as a more complicated forecasting model. I should point out that as I write this, there are five Democratic and seventeen Republican candidates, and while it seems apparent who will be nominated to the Democratic ticket (though I wouldn't put money on it), the Republican ticket is anybody's guess.

3. Though French sociologist Auguste Comte is usually credited with the first use of the phrase, it appears that the French term *démographie* did not exist until shortly before Comte's death and also that the first contemporary use of the term was actually in Scammon and Wattenberg's (1970) *The Real Majority* to describe important demographic correlates of voting behavior (Weeks 2013).

REFERENCES

Abramowitz, Alan I. 2010. *The Disappearing Center.* New Haven: Yale University Press.

Abramowitz, Alan I., and Kyle L. Saunders. 1998. "Ideological Realignment in the US Electorate." *Journal of Politics* 60(3): 634–52.

Abramowitz, Alan I., and Kyle L. Saunders. 2008. "Is Polarization a Myth?" *Journal of Politics* 70: 542–55.

Abramowitz, Alan, and Ruy Teixeira. 2009. "The Decline of the White Working Class and the Rise of a Mass Upper-Middle Class." *Political Science Quarterly* 124(3): 391–422.

Adams, Greg D. 1997. "Abortion: Evidence of an Issue Evolution." *American Journal of Political Science* 41(3): 718–37.

Agnew, John. 1996. "Mapping Politics: How Context Counts in Electoral Geography." *Political Geography* 15(2): 129–46.

Ardoin, Phillip J. 2009. "Exploring Partisan Bias in the Electoral College, 1964–2008." *White House Studies* 9(4): 331–44.

Bafumi, Joseph, and Robert Y. Shapiro. 2009. "A New Partisan Voter." *Journal of Politics* 71(1): 1–24.

Barreto, Matt A., Loren Collingwood, and Sylvia Manzano. 2010. "A New Measure of Group Influence in Presidential Elections: Assessing Latino Influence in 2008." *Political Research Quarterly* 63(4): 908–21.

Berelson, Bernard, Paul F. Lazarsfeld, and William McPhee. 1954. *Voting: A Study of Opinion Formation in a Presidential Campaign.* Chicago: University of Chicago Press.

Bernstein, Jonathan. 2012. "Do Democrats Have a Permanent Electoral College Advantage?" *salon.com*, http://www.salon.com/2012/12/01/do_democrats_have_a_permanent_electoral_college_advantage/. Accessed March 27, 2014.

Berry, William D., et al. 2010. "Measuring Citizen and Government Ideology in the U.S. States: A Re-Appraisal." *State Politics & Policy Quarterly* 10(2): 117–35.

Berry, William D., Evan J. Ringquist, Richard C. Fording, and Russell L. Hanson. 1998. "Measuring Citizen and Government Ideology in the American States, 1960–93." *American Journal of Political Science* 42(1): 327.

Bishop, Bill. 2009. *The Big Sort.* New York: Houghton Mifflin Harcourt.

Black, Merle. 2004. "The Transformation of the Southern Democratic Party." *Journal of Politics* 66(4): 1001–17.

Black, Merle, and Earl Black. 2009. *The Rise of Southern Republicans*. Cambridge, MA: Harvard University Press.

Box-Steffensmeier, Janet M., Suzanna De Boef, and Tse-min Lin. 2004. "The Dynamics of the Partisan Gender Gap." *American Political Science Review* 98(3): 515–28.

Brewer, Mark D., and Jeffrey M. Stonecash. 2006. *Split: Class and Cultural Divides in American Politics*. Washington, DC: CQ Press.

Brookes, R. H. 1960. "The Analysis of Distorted Representation in Two-Party Single-Member Elections." *Political Science* 12(2): 158–67.

Brooks, Clem, and Jeff Manza. 1997a. "Partisan Alignments of the 'Old' and 'New' Middle Classes in Post-Industrial America." In *Citizen Politics in Post-Industrial Societies*, ed. Terry Nichols Clark and Michael Rempel. Boulder, CO: Westview Press, 143–57.

Brooks, Clem, and Jeff Manza. 1997b. "Social Cleavages and Political Alignments: U.S. Presidential Elections, 1960 to 1992." *American Sociological Review* 62(6): 937–46.

Brown, Thad A. 1988. *Migration and Politics*. Chapel Hill: University of North Carolina Press.

Brunk, Gregory G., and Paul A. Gough. 1983. "State Economic Conditions and the 1980 Presidential Election." *Presidential Studies Quarterly* 13: 62–69.

Bullock, Charles S., Donna R. Hoffman, and Ronald Keith Gaddie. 2006. "Regional Variations in the Realignment of American Politics, 1944–2004." *Social Science Quarterly* 87: 494–518.

Bullock, John G. 2011. "Elite Influence on Public Opinion in an Informed Electorate." *American Political Science Review* 105(03): 496–515.

Burbank, Matthew J. 1997. "Explaining Contextual Effects on Vote Choice." *Political Behavior* 19(2): 113–32.

Burmila, Edward M. 2009. "The Electoral College after Census 2010 and 2020: The Political Impact of Population Growth and Redistribution." *Perspectives on Politics* 7: 837–47.

Burnham, Walter Dean. 1970. *Critical Elections and the Mainsprings of American Politics*. New York: Norton.

Burns, Alexander. 2013. "Dems Launch Plan to Turn Texas Blue." *politico.com*, http://social.politico.com/story/2013/01/democrats-launch-plan-to-turn-texas-blue-86651.html. Accessed March 27, 2014.

Buttice, Matthew K., and Benjamin Highton. 2013. "How Does Multilevel Regression and Poststratification Perform with Conventional National Surveys?" *Political Analysis* 21: 449–67.

Campbell, Angus A., Philip E. Converse, Warren E. Miller, and Donald E. Stokes. 1960. *The American Voter*. Chicago: University of Chicago Press.

Campbell, James E. 1992. "Forecasting the Presidential Vote in the States." *American Journal of Political Science* 36(2): 386.

Carmines, Edward G., Jessica C. Gerrity, and Michael W. Wagner. 2010. "How Abortion Became a Partisan Issue: Media Coverage of the Interest Group–Political Party Connection." *Politics & Policy* 38(6): 1135–58.

Carmines, Edward G., and James A. Stimson. 1989. *Issue Evolution*. Princeton, NJ: Princeton University Press.

Carsey, Thomas M., and Jeffrey J. Harden. 2010. "New Measures of Partisanship, Ideology, and Policy Mood in the American States." *State Politics & Policy Quarterly* 10(2): 136–56.

Chaney, Carol Kennedy, R. Michael Alvarez, and Jonathon Nagler. 1998. "Explaining the Gender Gap in U.S. Presidential Elections, 1980–1992." *Political Research Quarterly* 51(2): 311.

Clawson, Rosalee A., and Zoe M. Oxley. 2012. *Public Opinion: Democratic Ideals, Democratic Practice*. Washington, DC: CQ Press.

Coan, Travis G., and Mirya R. Holman. 2008. "Voting Green." *Social Science Quarterly* 89(5): 1121–35.

Collingwood, Loren, Matt A. Barreto, and Sergio I. Garcia-Rios. 2014. "Revisiting Latino Voting: Cross-Racial Mobilization in the 2012 Election." *Political Research Quarterly* 67(3): 632–45.

Delli Carpini, Michael X., and Scott Keeter. 1997. *What Americans Know about Politics and Why It Matters*. New Haven: Yale University Press.

DeSart, Jay A., and Thomas M. Holbrook. 2003. "Statewide Trial-Heat Polls and the 2000 Presidential Election: A Forecast Model." *Social Science quarterly* 84(3): 561–73.

Destler, I. M. 1996. "The Myth of the 'ElectoralLock'." *PS: Political Science & Politics* 29: 491–94.

de Vos, Sjoerd. 1998. "The Analysis of Compositional Effects as Exemplified by the Study of Elections." *GeoJournal* 44(1): 43–49.

Disarro, Brian, Jillian Barber, and Tom W. Rice. 2007. "Elections: The Home State Effect in Presidential Elections. Advances in the Study of Localism." *Presidential Studies Quarterly* 37(3): 558–66.

Enns, Peter K., and Julianna Koch. 2013. "Public Opinion in the US States 1956 to 2010." *State Politics & Policy Quarterly* 13: 349–72.

Feldman, Stanley, and Christopher Johnston. 2014. "Understanding the Determinants of Political Ideology: Implications of Structural Complexity." *Political Psychology* 35(3): 337–58.

Fiorina, Morris P., Samuel J. Abrams, and Jeremy C. Pope. 2004. *Culture War? The Myth of a Polarized America*. New York: Pearson.

Florida, Richard. 2004. *The Rise of the Creative Class and How It's Transforming Work, Leisure, Community and Everyday Life*. New York: Basic Books.

Gelman, Andrew. 2015. "How Better Educated Whites Are Driving Political Polarization." In *Political Polarization in American Politics*, ed. Daniel J. Hopkins and John Sides. New York: Bloomsbury Academic, 91–94.

Gelman, Andrew, et al. 2008. *Red State, Blue State, Rich State, Poor State*. Princeton, NJ: Princeton University Press.

Gerskoff, Amy. 2009. "The Marriage Gap." In *Beyond Red State, Blue State: Electoral Gaps in the Twenty-First Century American Electorate*, ed. Laura R. Olson and John C. Green. New York: Pearson Prentice Hall, 24–39.

Gimpel, James G., and Jason E. Schuknecht. 2001. "Interstate Migration and Electoral Politics." *Journal of Politics* 63(1): 207–31.

Gimpel, James G, and Jason E Schuknecht. 2004. *Patchwork Nation: Sectionalism and Political Change in American Politics*. Ann Arbor: University of Michigan Press.

Gluek, Katie. 2014. "Paul Warns Texas Could Turn Blue." *Politico*, February 9, http://www.politico.com/story/2014/02/rand-paul-texas-could-turn-blue-103292.html. Accessed March 27, 2014.

Green, John C., and Laura R. Olson. 2009. "'Gapology' and the 2004 Presidential Vote." In *Beyond Red State, Blue State: Electoral Gaps in the Twenty-First Century Electorate*, ed. Laura R. Olson and John C. Green. New York: Pearson Prentice Hall, 1–9.

Hansford, Thomas G., and Brad Gomez. 2010. "Estimating the Electoral Effects of Voter Turnout." *American Political Science Review* 104(2): 268–88.

Hayes, Danny, and Seth C. McKee. 2008. "Toward a One-Party South?" *American Politics Research* 36(1): 3–32.

Herr, J. Paul. 2008. "The Impact of Campaign Appearances in the 1996 Election." *Journal of Politics* 64(3): 904–13.

Hetherington, Marc. 2001. "Resurgent Mass Partisanship: The Role of Elite Polarization." *American Political Science Review* 95(3): 619–31.

Hirsch, Barry, and David MacPherson. 2014. "Union Membership and Coverage Database from the Current Population Survey." unionstats.com. Accessed April 16, 2014.

Hogan, Robert E. 2004. "Challenger Emergence, Incumbent Success, and Electoral Accountability in State Legislative Elections." *Journal of Politics* 66(4): 1283–1303.

Holbrook, Thomas M. 1991. "Presidential Elections in Space and Time." *American Journal of Political Science* 35(1): 91–109.

Holbrook, Thomas M., and Aaron C. Weinschenk. 2014. "Money, Candidates, and Mayoral Elections." *Electoral Studies* 35: 292–302.

Holbrook, Thomas, and Brianne Heidbreder. 2010. "Does Measurement Matter? The Case of VAP and VEP in Models of Voter Turnout in the United States." *State Politics & Policy Quarterly* 10(2): 157–79.

Holbrook, Thomas M., and Scott D. McClurg. 2005. "The Mobilization of Core Supporters: Campaigns, Turnout, and Electoral Composition in United States Presidential Elections." *American Journal of Political Science* 49(4): 689–703.

Holbrook, Thomas M., and Steven C. Poe. 1987. "Measuring State Political Ideology." *American Politics Research* 15(3): 399–415.

Hood, M. V., and S. C. McKee. 2010. "What Made Carolina Blue? In-Migration and the 2008 North Carolina Presidential Vote." *American Politics Research* 38(2): 266–302.

Hout, Michael, Jeff Manza, and Clem Brooks. 1999. "Classes, Unions, and the Realignment of US Presidential Voting, 1952–1992." In *The End of Class Politics?*, ed. Geoffery Evans. New York: Oxford University Press, 183–96.

Houtman, Dick. 2001. "Class, Culture, and Conservatism: Reassessing Education as a Variable in Political Sociology." In *The Breakdown of Class Politics*, ed. Terry Nichols Clark and Seymour Martin Lipset. Washington, DC: Woodrow Wilson Center Press, 161–95.

Huckfeldt, Robert, Eric Plutzer, and John Sprague. 1993. "Alternative Contexts of Political Behavior: Churches, Neighborhoods, and Individuals." *Journal of Politics* 55(2): 365–81.

Imai, Kosuke, and Gary King. 2004. "Did Illegal Overseas Absentee Ballots Decide the 2000 U.S. Presidential Election?" *Perspectives on Politics* 2(3): 537–49.

Jacobson, Gary C. 2012. *The Politics of Congressional Elections.* 8th ed. New York: Pearson Higher Ed.

Johnston, Ron, Charles Pattie, and David Rossiter. 2001. "He Lost . . . but He Won! Electoral Bias and George W. Bush's Victory in the US Presidential Election, 2000." *Representation* 38(2): 150–58.

Judis, John B., and Ruy Teixeira. 2004. *The Emerging Democratic Majority.* New York: Simon and Schuster.

Jurjevich, Jason R., and David A. Plane. 2012. "Voters on the Move: The Political Effectiveness of Migration and Its Effects on State Partisan Composition." *Political Geography* 31(7): 429–43.

Kahn, Matthew E. 2002. "Demographic Change and the Demand for Environmental Regulation." *Journal of Policy Analysis and Management* 21(1): 45–62.

Kaufmann, Karen M. 2002. "Culture Wars, Secular Realignment, and the Gender Gap in Party Identification." *Political Behavior* 24(3): 283–307.

———. 2009. "The Gender Gap." In *Beyond Red State, Blue State: Electoral Gaps in the Twenty-First Century American Electorate,* ed. Laura R. Olson and John C. Green. New York: Pearson Prentice Hall, 92–108.

Kaufmann, Karen M., and John R. Petrocik. 1999. "The Changing Politics of American Men: Understanding the Sources of the Gender Gap." *American Journal of Political Science* 43(3): 864.

Key, V. O. 1955. "A Theory of Critical Elections." *Journal of Politics* 17(1): 3–18.

———. 1959. "Secular Realignment and the Party System." *Journal of Politics* 21: 198–210.

Kinder, Donald R., and Lynn M. Sanders. 1996. *Divided by Color.* Chicago: University of Chicago Press.

King, James D. 2001. "Incumbent Popularity and Vote Choice in Gubernatorial Elections." *Journal of Politics* 63(2): 585–97.

Knuckey, Jonathan. 2009. "Explaining Partisan Change among Northeastern Whites." *Politics & Policy* 37(6): 1331–55.

Kornacki, Steve. 2012. "When Gender Gaps Save Presidents." *Salon,* April 2, http://www.salon.com/2012/04/02/when_gender_gaps_save_presidents/. Accessed April 15, 2015.

Krebs, Timothy B. 1998. "The Determinants of Candidates' Vote Share and the Advantages of Incumbency in City Council Elections." *American Journal of Political Science* 42: 921–35.

Ladd, Chris. 2014. "The Missing Story of the 2014 Election." *Chron.com,* November 10, http://blog.chron.com/goplifer/2014/11/the-missing-story-of-the-2014-election/#28114101=0. Accessed December 3, 2014.

Lax, Jeffrey R., and Justin H. Phillips. 2009. "How Should We Estimate Public Opinion in the States?" *American Journal of Political Science* 53(1): 107–21.

Lazarsfeld, Paul F., Bernard Berelson, and Hazel Gaudet. 1944. *The People's Choice: How the Voter Makes Up His Mind in a Presidential Campaign.* New York: Columbia University Press.

Leege, David C., and Lyman A. Kellstedt. 1993. *Rediscovering the Religious Factor in American Politics.* New York: M. E. Sharpe.

Leege, David C., Kenneth D. Wald, Brian S. Krueger, and Paul D. Mueller. 2002. *The Politics of Cultural Differences*. Princeton, NJ: Princeton University Press.

Levendusky, Matthew. 2009. *The Partisan Sort*. Chicago: University of Chicago Press.

———. 2010. "Clearer Cues, More Consistent Voters: A Benefit of Elite Polarization." *Political Behavior* 32(1): 111–31.

Liere, Kent D. Van, and Riley E. Dunlap. 1980. "The Social Bases of Environmental Concern: A Review of Hypotheses, Explanations and Empirical Evidence." *Public Opinion Quarterly* 44(2): 181–97.

Lorinskas, Robert A., Brett W. Hawkins, and Steven D. Edwards. 1969. "The Persistence of Ethnic Voting in Urban and Rural Areas: Results from the Controlled Election Method." *Social Science Quarterly* 49(4): 891–99.

MacDonald, Jason A., and William W. Franko. 2008. "What Moves Partisanship? Migration, State Partisan Environment Change, and Party Identification." *American Politics Research* 36(6): 880–902.

Manza, Jeff, and Clem Brooks. 1999. *Social Cleavages and Political Change: Voter Alignments and U.S. Party Coalitions*. New York: Oxford University Press.

Marsh, Michael. 2002. "Electoral Context." *Electoral Studies* 21(2): 207–17.

Mayhew, David R. 1974. "Congressional Elections: The Case of the Vanishing Marginals." *Polity* 6(3): 295–317.

Mayhew, David R. 2001. "Electoral Realignments." *Annual Review of Political Science* 3(1): 449–74.

———. 2002. *Electoral Realignments: A Critique of an American Genre*. New Haven: Yale University Press.

McCarty, Nolan M., Keith T. Poole, and Howard Rosenthal. 2006. *Polarized America: The Dance of Ideology and Unequal Riches*. Cambridge, MA: MIT Press.

McClerking, Harwood. 2009. "Racial and Ethnic Gaps." In *Beyond Red State, Blue State: Electoral Gaps in the Twenty-First Century American Electorate*, ed. Laura R. Olson and John C. Green. New York: Pearson Prentice Hall, 10–23.

McDonald, Michael, and Samuel L. Popkin. 2001. "The Myth of the Vanishing Voter." *American Political Science Review* 95(4): 963–74.

McKee, Seth C., and Jeremy M. Teigen. 2009. "Probing the Reds and Blues: Sectionalism and Voter Location in the 2000 and 2004 U.S. Presidential Elections." *Political Geography* 28(8): 484–95.

Meffert, Michael F., Helmut Norpoth, and Anirudh V. Ruhil. 2001. "Realignment and Macropartisanship." *American Political Science Review* 95(4): 953–62.

Milkis, Sidney M., Daniel J. Tichenor, and Laura Blessing. 2013. "'Rallying Force': The Modern Presidency, Social Movements, and the Transformation of American Politics." *Presidential Studies Quarterly* 43(3): 641–70.

Miller, Warren E. 1991. "Party Identification, Realignment, and Party Voting: Back to the Basics." *American Political Science Review* 85(2): 557.

Miller, Warren Edward, and J. Merrill Shanks. 1996. *The New American Voter*. Cambridge, MA: Harvard University Press.

Murphy, Mike, and Trent Wisecup. 2013. "Guest Commentary: Michigan Can Be Testing Ground for a Refocused GOP." *Detroit Free Press*, April 7, http://www.freep.com/article/20130407/OPINION05/304070083/1068/rss06. Accessed October 23, 2014.

Olson, Laura R., and John C. Green. 2006. "The Religion Gap." *PS: Political Science & Politics* 39(3): 455–59.

Olson, Laura R., and John Clifford Green. 2008. *Beyond Red State, Blue State.* New York: Prentice Hall.

Oppenheimer, Bruce I., James A. Stimson, and Richard W. Waterman. 1986. "Interpreting U.S. Congressional Elections: The Exposure Thesis." *Legislative Studies Quarterly* 11(2): 227–47.

Ortiz, Hector L., and Jeffrey M. Stonecash. 2009. "The Class Gap." In *Beyond Red State, Blue State: Electoral Gaps in the Twenty-First Century American Electorate,* ed. Laura R. Olson and John C. Green. New York: Pearson Prentice Hall, 53–73.

Pacheco, Julianna. 2011. "Using National Surveys to Measure Dynamic U.S. State Public Opinion: A Guideline for Scholars and an Application." *State Politics & Policy Quarterly* 15: 436–66.

Pattie, Charles, and Ron Johnston. 2014. "'The Electors Shall Meet in Their Respective States': Bias and the US Presidential Electoral College, 1960–2012." *Political Geography* 40: 35–45.

Petrocik, John R. 1981. *Party Coalitions: Realignments and the Decline of the New Deal Party System.* Chicago: University of Chicago Press.

———. 1987. "Realignment: New Party Coalitions and the Nationalization of the South." *Journal of Politics* 49(2): 347–75.

Pieper, Andrew L. 2011. "Flouting Faith? Religious Hostility and the American Left, 1977–2000." *American Politics Research* 39(4): 754–78.

Plutzer, Eric, and Michael McBurnett. 1991. "Family Life and American Politics: The Marriage Gap Reconsidered." *Public Opinion Quarterly* 55(1): 113–27.

Pomper, Gerald. 1966. "Ethnic and Group Voting in Nonpartisan Municipal Elections." *Public Opinion Quarterly* 30(1): 79–97.

———. 1967. "Classification of Presidential Elections." *Journal of Politics* 29(3): 535–66.

Poole, Keith T., and Howard Rosenthal. 1985. "A Spatial Model for Legislative Roll Call Analysis." *American Journal of Political Science* 29(2): 357–84.

Popkin, Samuel. 1994. *The Reasoning Voter: Communication and Persuasion in Presidential Campaigns.* 2nd ed. Chicago: University of Chicago Press.

Prysby, Charles, and John Books. 1987. "Modeling Contextual Effects on Political Behavior: Static versus Dynamic Models." *Political Behavior* 9(3): 225–45.

Rabinowitz, George, Stuart Elaine Macdonald, and Paul-Henri Gurian. 1984. "The Structure of Presidential Elections and the Process of Realignment, 1944 to 1980." *American Journal of Political Science* 28(4): 611.

Ramakrishnan, S. Karthick. 2014. "Asian Americans and the Rainbow: The Prospects and Limits of Coalitional Politics." *Politics, Groups, and Identities* 2(3): 522–29.

———. 2015. "Voting: Key Figures." AAPI Data, aapidata.com/civic/voting.

Robinson, Tony, and Stephen Noriega. 2010. "Voter Migration as a Source of Electoral Change in the Rocky Mountain West." *Political Geography* 29(1): 28–39.

Robinson, William S. 1950. "Ecological Correlations and the Behavior of Individuals." *American Sociological Review* 15: 351–57.

Rosenstone, Steven J. 1983. *Forecasting Presidential Elections.* New Haven: Yale University Press.

Ruggles, Steven, et al. "Integrated Public Use Microdata Series: Version 5.0 [Machine-Readable Database]." IPUMS USA, https://usa.ipums.org/usa/.

Scammon, Richard M., and Ben J. Wattenberg. 1970. *The Real Majority*. New York: Coward-McCann.

Segura, Gary M. 2012. "Latino Public Opinion and Realigning the American Electorate." *Daedalus* 141(4): 98.

Shaw, Daron R. 2008. *The Race to 270: The Electoral College and the Campaign Strategies of 2000 and 2004*. Chicago: University of Chicago Press.

Silver, Nate. 2012. "As Nation and Parties Change, Republicans Are at an Electoral College Disadvantage." *fivethirtyeight.blogs.nytimes*, http://fivethirtyeight.blogs.nytimes.com/2012/11/08/as-nation-and-parties-change-republicans-are-at-an-electoral-college-disadvantage/. Accessed March 27, 2014.

Soumbatiants, Souren, Henry W. ChappellJr, and Eric Johnson. 2006. "Using State Polls to Forecast U.S. Presidential Election Outcomes." *Public Choice* 127(1–2): 207–23.

Stanford University and University of Michigan. 2014. "American National Election Studies: Time Series Cumulative Data File, 1948–2012." September 25 release. http://www.electionstudies.org/studypages/cdf/anes_timeseries_cdf.htm.

Stephanopoulos, Nicholas O., and Eric M. McGehee. 2015. "Partisan Gerrymandering and the Efficiency Gap." *University of Chicago Law Review* 82: 831–900.

Stimson, James A. 2004. *Tides of Consent*. Cambridge, UK: Cambridge University Press.

Tesler, Michael, and David O. Sears. 2010. *Obama's Race*. Chicago: University of Chicago Press.

Wand, Jonathan N. et al. 2001. "The Butterfly Did It: The Aberrant Vote for Buchanan in Palm Beach County, Florida." *American Political Science Review* 95(4): 793–810.

Weeks, John. 2013. "The Origins of 'Demography Is Destiny' Revealed." *Weeks Population*, November 13, http://weekspopulation.blogspot.com/2013/11/the-origins-of-demography-is-destiny.html. Accessed July 30, 2015.

Weinschenk, Aaron C. 2014. "Polarization, Ideology, and Vote Choice in US Congressional Elections." *Journal of Elections, Public Opinion and Parties* 24(1): 73–89.

Weisberg, Herbert F. 1987. "The Demographics of a New Voting Gap: Marital Differences in American Voting." *Public Opinion Quarterly* 51(3): 335.

Wright, Gerald C., Robert S. Erikson, and John P. McIver. 1985. "Measuring State Partisanship and Ideology with Survey Data." *Journal of Politics* 47(2): 469–89.

Zaller, John. 1991. "Information, Values, and Opinion." *American Political Science Review* 85(4): 1215–37.